INDEPENDENT RESEARCH NETWORK

I0110295

ANTHROPOLOGY ACROSS BORDERS AND LIMITS: 1ST INDEPENDENT RESEARCH NETWORK PAPERS

PROCEEDINGS FROM THE 3RD-5TH RUSSIAN-AMERICAN RESEARCH NEXUS FORUMS

EDITED BY
Roman N. Ignatiev and Vladislav V. Fediushin

IRN

Meabooks, Inc • 2023

This volume presents a collection of papers on New World anthropology and history, from physical anthropology to historical memory to women's history. The papers were presented at the 3rd, 4th, and 5th Russian-American Research Nexus (RARN) Forums, and offer a unique perspective on the New World from a variety of Russian and American scholars.

This book will be of interest to students and scholars of anthropology and history ofthe New World. It is also an essential resource for anyone interested in the latest research on this important topic.

ISBN 978-1-988391-20-5

Table of Contents

Craniological Characteristics of the Indians of South America and Their Comparison with the Populations of the Old World

Alexandra A. Castro Stepanova, Olga A. Fedorchuk

Introduction

The origin and processes of formation of the indigenous po-pu-lation of the New World have long been of interest to various researchers. There are quite a lot of works devoted to the study of the morphology of skulls from these territories. Some of these works are of a generalizing, summary nature.

One of the earliest hypotheses about the origin of the indige-nous populations of America was that it was settled by people who had features of an unformed Asian complex of characters (Rogin-sky 1937; Howells 1940). According to some bioanthropological and linguistic evidence, the settlement of America began between 35000–30000 years ago, with protomorphic Asian populations that had features similar to the Western Siberian populations (such as Kets, Khanty, Mansi). Later, perhaps not finding any competitors on the American continent, they underwent an adaptive radiation that led to the occupation of all ecological niches, including Tierra del Fuego (Rodríguez 1987). Following, presumably, from the more northern regions of Asia, some other populations — native speakers of the Na-Dene language — penetrated the American continent. As a result of evolutionary processes that had already taken place in Asia, these populations were estimated to be about 85% Mongoloid. This gene flow influenced the genetic structure of the Indians of North America and parts of Central America, increasing the Mongoloids proportion. The third wave of migrations from the territory of Asia is the one of the 100% Mongoloid Eskimo-Aleutian populations (Rodríguez, 1987, p. 35). "The whole process of the formation of Americanoids is unique, although at different stages it reveals features that later developed in the Old World into the Australoid and Mongoloid complexes. in the modern classification, Amerindians should take a special place" (Zubov 1999: 42–43).

In later works, this assumption is refined. First, it is said that the skull morphology of the early inhabitants of South and Mesoamerica (and, possibly, North America) was very different from that which can be observed in more recent series (Neves and Hubbe 2005). While the skulls of the modern indigenous population are characterized by a short and wide rearly Southern and Mesoamericans was different. They had a long and narrow brain region, a low and protruding face, and low orbits and nose (Neves and Hubbe 2005). Two different scenarios have been proposed to explain these morphological changes: (a) the penetration of two very different biological populations into the New World during the final Pleistocene/Early Holocene through Beringia, and (b) a local microevolutionary process mimicking that which occurred in East Asia at that time. The first hypothesis seems more likely to the authors (Neves et al. 2007).

Another work also states that, apparently, several migration waves had taken place in different periods. The first wave mainly formed the population of Central and South America, the second — the population of the Northwest coast of the United States, and the third — the Aleuts and Eskimos. The first people who settled the New World were more similar to the Pacific populations than to the Australo-Melanesian ones (Rodríguez 2007).

These conclusions are supported by another work, which shows that, based on a comparison of the total characteristics of the Amerindian cranial series, they are most similar to the populations of East and Southeast Asia (Pestryakov, Grigorieva 2009). Apparently the first main wave of the ancient settlement of America came from the territory of East Asia. Groups from the territory of America are distinguished by significant craniological diversity: "The earliest groups of migrants to America, who best preserved their special craniotype, are territorially the most distant from Beringia. These are the Indians of the extreme south of South America (central pampas, Patagonia and Tierra del Fuego). They are distinguished by a huge size of the skull, close to the maximum in the modern population of the Earth" (Pestryakov, Grigorieva 2009). According to the results of this study, the eastern groups have features indicating similarities with the Australo-Melanesian groups, which is interpreted as an indication of an older formation. There is a tendency to brachycephalization among the agricultural population.

Quite a long time ago, a clear geographical division of skull sizes was shown: the largest heads in the East and Southeast, and the smallest ones in the West and Northwest (Newman, Stewart 1950). At the same time, it was shown that over time, microevolutionary processes took place on the American continent, which were accompanied, among other things, by a change in the morphological features of the skull. According to one of the hypotheses, the main cause of these changes are climatic factors, the influence of which is described by the Bergman rule (Newman 1962). Basically, these conclusions are based on changes in growth: "It seems that the tall modern Indians in colder regions are descended from shorter ancestors. On the contrary, shorter modern Indians from areas with warmer climates had taller ancestors." (Ibid.: 253). Almost all the skulls of the ancient 'Paleo-Indian', as well as the skulls of the 'Archaic' period, which have not been subjected to artificial deformation, are moderately dolichocranial. But in every area of the New World, there is a trend towards brachycrania. This trend begins in the archaic period and is expressed in an average increase in the cranial index. By all indications, brachycrania and the associated changes in the cranial vault, base, and face are evolutionary in nature, although the mechanism of this phenomenon is not understood" (Ibid.: 253). in some works, the same process is associated with the transition of the population to settled agriculture, at least for the populations of Mesoamerica and the Central Andes (Rodríguez 1987).

The relatively modern population of North America is classified roughly as follows:

1. Circumarctic (Eskimos and Aleuts);

2. Pacific, including the Na-Dene language group (Atabaskan, 3. Tlingit, Haida, Apache, Pueblo);

4. North Atlantic, "Algonquian" (Sioux, Blackfoot, Ponca, Arikara, Huron, Cheyenne);

The Central-South American complex is also divided into options:

1. Central American (including part of the Indians of the modern southern regions of the USA);

2. Circumcaribbean (Indians of modern territories of northern Colombia, Venezuela, Guyana, Suriname, Antilles);

3. Andean regions of Colombia, Ecuador, Peru, Bolivia, Chile;

4. Southern variant (Argentine pampa, Tierra del Fuego, part of Chile, Bolivia and the Amazonian basin;

5. The Amazonian variant, the material on which is very scarce, so that one can only judge a significant heterogeneity and influx of genes from the Circum-Caribbean, Andean and southern regions (Rodriguez 1983, cited in: Rodriguez 1987)

The purpose of this work was to create the most reliable and complete generalization of the available craniometric data on the Indians of South America and the comparison of these data on a wide scale of intergroup variability. For this, comparative data from the territory of North America, as well as from the eastern regions of the Old World (Asia, Australia, Oceania) were used.

Materials

Materials from the territory of North America
For this study, data were drawn on 16 groups from the territory of North America from A. Hrdlicka (1927, 1940). The groups and number of individuals in each one are listed in Table 2.

Materials from the territory of South America
In total, 17 ethno-territorial groups from the territory of South America were studied (Table 1). Three from Argentina, two from Brazil, one from Venezuela, five from Peru, two from Chile and four from Tierra del Fuego.

Argentina
From Argentina, we studied two groups of Patagonians, one from the territory of Rio Negro, and one from Rio Chubut (Marelli 1913). The Rio Negro series of skulls consists of ancient Patagonian skulls, to which are added Martin's measurements of other Patagonians (Martin 1896), as well as copies of the

Museum of Natural History of Buenos Aires, which Dr. Florentino Ameguinho allowed measured in 1910. The second series included 100 Patagonian skulls, exhumed from the cemeteries of the Chubut River Valley, which entered the collection of the La Plata Museum in 1893.

Brazil

From Brazil, 2 series were included in the analysis.

1) The first one is the measurements of skulls of the Botocudo people taken from 3 sources.

From the work of Philippe Marius Rey (1880), we got data on 6 Botocudo skulls, where 2 male skulls belong to individuals of the Potons village tribe, Mucuri river valley. These 2 skulls, along with the skeleton of Botocudo and many other Brazilian aboriginal skulls, were sent by the Emperor of Brazil to the Museum of Natural History. The other 4 Botocudo skulls (where 2 are of females) were exhumed by the author from the right bank of the Doce River, belonging to a tribe that disappeared after colonization. These 4 skulls have been donated to the Anthropological Society. All skulls are in excellent condition.

J. Rodrigues Peixoto (1885) also studied the Botocudo tribe and their mestization with Europeans. We used only the data of the not mixed-breed males (6 skulls), kept at that time in the National Museum of Brazil. They are of different origin — one from San Matheus (Espirito Santo), given to the author by a friend who dug it out of an old Indian cemetery. Two are from the Dosi river valley — one of an old man, and one of an adult. Another 3 skulls were collected by the geologist Carlos Hartt in the Mucuri river valley, but he left no geological context that could allow us to understand the period in which these people lived. Nonetheless, it is believed that these skulls are quite ancient, as they are characterized by "archaic" (or classical) features, which are smoothed out in later groups due mestization.

The third source of Botocudo data comes from the work of Dr. Paul Ehrenreich (1887). He studies 13 skulls that he found from 3 sources, but, unfortunately, besides the place of origin not much information is given.

2) The second group studied from Brazil is the Lagoa Santa series (Rivet 1908). The studied series consists of 17 skulls, 15 of which belong to the Zoological Museum of Copenhagen, 1 to the Museum of Natural History in London and 1 to the Museum of Rio de Janeiro. Unfortunately, the exact dating of the human remains found by Lund (these are those in Copenhagen) is impossible. It was collected in 1843 in a cave in the province of Minas Gerais (Brazil), not far from Lagoa Santa. For the other 2 skulls no information was provided.

Venezuela

We used data on 53 skulls (Zamakona de Arechavaleta, Lagrange de Castillo 2007) from two states of Venezuela: Aragua and Carabobo, which are currently stored in the Adolfo Ernst Center at the Museum of Natural Sciences of Caracas. Eight cranioscopic features were analyzed, which noted the degree of development and prominence of different areas, as well as the overall stoutness of each skull, in order to determine the existing differences in terms of sexual dimorphism. Sex was determined for 49 skulls, of which 24 were male and 25 females. For the remaining 4 skulls, gender could not be assigned. The skulls of both sexes tend to be brachycephalic. Most of the undeformed skulls were classified as low to medium height, and the deformed skulls were all of low height. Prognathism is more pronounced in non-deformed skulls than in the deformed ones. The volume of the skull, as practice has shown, does not depend on the deformation. Both undeformed and deformed skulls were of small volume, with a tendency to microcephaly.

Table 1. Arithmetic mean values of craniometric traits in different groups from the territory of South America.

№	Region	Group	Source	n
1	Argentina	Patagonians (Rio Negro)	Martin, 1896	117
2		Parana		44
3		Patagonians (Rio Chubut)		56
4	Brazil	Botocudos	Rey, 1880; Peixoto, 1885; Ehreinreich, 1887	19
5		Lagoa Santa	Rivet, 1980	11
6	Venezuela	Valencia lake	Zamakona de Arechavaleta, Lagrange de Castillo, 2007	24
7	Tierra del Fuego	Ona	Hernandez, 1997	50
8		Yagan		42
9		Alakalufe	Own data	22
10			Hernandez, 1997	15
11	Peru	Calca	Ericksen, 1962	29
12		San Damian	Newman, 1943	67
13		Maqui maqui	Ericksen, 1962	8
14		Paucarcancha		117
15		Chicama	Stewart,1943	65
16	Chile	Araucano	Latcham, 1904	14
17		Mapuche	Own Data	16

* For explanation refer to the "Methods" section.

Table 1. Arithmetic mean values of craniometric traits in different groups from the territory of South America.

Craniometric feature (by Martin's numeration) *										
M.1	M.8	M.17	M.5	M.9	M.10	M.40	M.48	M.45	M.54	M.55
182,8	141,3	143	100,6	94,1	110,2	102,4	74,5	140,1	25,1	53,7
186,2	142,7	146,9	104,0	95,0	–	102,0	76,7	144,6	26,1	55,8
185,5	146,2	141,5	105,9	97,7	115,8	104,8	75,9	148,8	25,6	54,1
183,6	136,3	139,9	103,5	92,4	98,0	–	71,5	137,7	24,8	52,9
182,0	129,7	134,6	101,4	93,9	112,6	–	67,9	136,6	25,6	49,6
177,0	142,3	127,1	96,6	95,4	106,2	100,6	73,3	137,6	24,6	57,3
191,3	143,1	136,6	103,7	–	116,2	101,3	–	143,5	–	55,4
186,3	142,9	136,0	102,8	–	116,9	101,8	–	143,3	24,9	54,0
184,7	142,3	134,6	–	93,9	116,6	–	75,5	139,6	–	–
188,3	142,1	137,9	102,8	–	115,2	101,9	–	141,0	–	56,1
175,1	135,4	134,9	97,6	90,5	–	94,5	66,8	135,0	24,8	52
177,6	139,7	132,2	94,8	90,8	–	92,0	72,0	135,7	24,0	50,3
182,4	135,4	131,0	98,0	94,1	–	96,7	68,2	137,8	24,1	48,8
179,4	135,5	137,1	98,6	92,3	–	96,1	67,8	133,9	24,3	49
176,1	139,7	135,3	98,5	92,1	–	97,1	67,4	135,3	24,6	48,7
175,5	140,7	137,2	–	98,5	120,6	–	–	136,3	25,4	52,6
175,2	143,6	134,8	–	91,6	116,9	–	68,2	141,9	–	–

Peru

Skulls from the territory of Peru have previously been studied by several researchers. The series used in these works have proper archaeological documentation, exclude skulls with artificial deformations, and are comparable in measurement methods with the ones used in the Russian anthropological school. The groups used are the following:

• Maqui-Maquis (Ericksen 1962) Eight male and six female skulls are from the site of Los Corredores de los Maqui-Maquis, 6 km northeast of the town of San Pablo. The pottery found near the remains puts them in the Cajamarca I or II culture in the years 100 BC – 400 AD.

• Paucarcancha (MacCurdy 1923). Late period male and female series from a series of caves such as Paucarcancha along the Urabamba drainage in the southern Peruvian highlands.

• Calca (Ericksen 1962).

• San Damian. Late period male and female series from the vicinity of the village of San Damian, Department of Huarochiri, in the central part of the Peruvian Highlands (US National Museum series measured by M.T. Newman (Newman 1943).

In terms of their location, the Paucarcancha and Calca samples are from the South Sierra, over 700 air miles south of Cajamarca. The San Damian sample is from the area of the Sierra just southeast of Lima, less than 500 air miles from Cajamarca.

• Chicama. Male and female series from the coastal Chicama Valley in northern Peru (Stewart 1943).

Hrdlicka (1911, 1914) was one of the first to distinguish the Coastal brachycephals from the more long-headed crania of the Sierra, and noted the occasional presence of the latter in Coastal cemeteries. Later, Newman (1948: 18) studied additional data and came to the conclusion that there are two racial varieties in the Sierra: the Central Intermontane, represented by the Paucarcancha sample and typified as "dolicho – low mesocephalic [...] high vaulted, medium-short faces, medium broad nasal apertures, very high orbits. Most characteristic is an oval vault contour, a low pinched occiput, flat temporals, low frontal, and rather low nasal root." (2) the Western Sierra, represented by the San Damian sample, and typically "mesocephalic [...], medium-vaulted, medium face, medium nasal aperture, barely high orbits. Most characteristic is the low pinched occiput, without the ovoid vault contour, flat temporals, and scaphocephaly of the Paucarcancha group." However, later works (Ericksen, 1962) show that the Calca sample is added to Newman's Central Intermontane variety and the Cajamarca samples are considered, they tend to blur any real sharpness of distinction between Newman's two Sierra varieties. If the suggestion that the Paucarcancha sample is pre-Inca were more secure, the differences with Calca which are the points of resemblance with San Damian could be attributed to time. Regretfully, since the dating of any of the samples is not reliable, these suggestions can only be taken as hypotheses.

Chile

From Chile, we used materials from Southern-Central groups: one from literature — the Araucanos (Latcham 1904), — and one group was measured by us: the Mapuche. There might be a bit of a confusion, because the Mapuche are part of the Araucanos. The race, to which the name of Araucano has been given, formerly populated the whole of Chile from the desert of Atacama, in the north, to the Island of Chiloe in the south. However, shortly after the Spanish conquest these groups were confined to the southern part of the country. The origin of the term Araucano is unknown, but it includes several smaller groups of peoples: *Moluches*, people of war, in the north; *Mapuches*, people of the land, in the provinces of Malleco and Cautin; *Pehuenches*, people of the pines, in the Andes valleys; and *Huilliches*, people of the south, in the provinces of Valdivia and Llanquihue. Latcham

obtained his data by living for three years in the province of Malleco and Cautin, where he was able to obtain abundant material
for a closer study. Artificial deformation of the skull is unknown
among these Indian. As a rule, they are sub-brachycephalic or
brachycephalic, hypsi- and akrocephalic in a high degree, phae-
nozygous, chamaeprosopic, platyopic, mesoseme, mesorhine,
prognathous, and ellipsoid. The first thing that one notices,
at a casual glance, is the broad face and trochocephalic form
of the skull, which looked at from any position presents a series
of rounded surface. There is also a narked prognathism, especially sub-nasal, and the supraciliary ridges and glabella are very
pronounced.

Author data on the Mapuche group was collected at the National Museum of Natural History in Santiago de Chile (Museo
Nacional de Historia Natural, Santiago, Chile). Craniological material relating to the Mapuche tribe was collected in the regions
of Araucania and Bio-Bio, in the central part of Chile. It mainly comes from the communes of Traiguén, Temuco, Arauco, and
Mulchen. This series approximately dates to the 10th–15th centuries. The series measured by the author includes 17 male and 16
female skulls.

Tierra del Fuego

From Tierra del Fuego, we included three groups. These are
the Alakalufs (also known as Kaweskar or Halakwulup), the Onas
(also known as Selk'nam), and the Yahgans (also known as Yamana).
Data on the three groups was taken from Hernandez et al. (1997).
All groups were hunter-gatherers that inhabited Tierra del Fuego before European contact. The Yahgan and the Alakalufs lived
on islands and channels of the Chilean Pacific coast and maintained occasional contacts with each other and also with the Pata-
gons who lived in the area north of the Magellan Straits. However,
the geographically marginal position of the Fueguian aborigines

with respect to the South American continent seems to have kept them apart from northern migratory movements. The samples from Tierra del Fuego used by the authors of the work include 180 skulls preserved at 14 different institutions, nine of them in South America and five in Europe. It is difficult to assign some Fueguian skulls to a specific aboriginal group, as was found during the 1880s and later with the appearance of interethnic mating. However, more than 90% of the skulls of Fueguians from European collections have individual information stored in museum records and are assigned to a specific aboriginal group. The percentages are similar for collections in South America, although it cannot be excluded that some specimens could be misplaced. From the authors' point of view, the distinct morphological pattern of Fueguians can be regarded as the consequence of both climatic and biomechanic adaptations and the geographic isolation of these groups may have contributed to the maintenance of a general morphological homogeneity within the Fueguian samples.

We also included data on the Alakalufs that was obtained by us at the National Museum of Natural History in Santiago de Chile. The skulls belonging to the representatives of the Alakaluf tribe come from the territory of the Tierra del Fuego archipelago, mainly from the island of Doson. However, there are also single finds from other islands of the archipelago — Navarino and Isla Grande (or Tierra del Fuego proper), — and also from the islands of the province of Magallanes. The skulls are tentatively dated to the 10th–15th centuries AD. This craniological series has been, apparently, repeatedly described, data on it were published by different authors (Newman 1943; Newman, Stewart 1950), and it is even included in the previously mentioned work (Hernandez, 1997), but for some reason the authors included data on only 15 males, while we obtained data on 22 males. Therefore, we decided to include this data in the study as well.

As a comparative material, 42 series from the territory of Asia

and Oceania were used (Table 2). From the territory of East,
Central, and North Asia, 27 series; 11 series, from Southeast and
South Asia; 4 series, from Australia and Oceania.

Table 2. List of groups used in the analysis and their affiliation to geographical communities (macroregions).

Macro-region	№	Ethno-territorial group	n	Source
North, Central, and Central Asia	1	Kazakhs	119	Ismagulov, 1970
	2	Telengits	55	own data
	3	Chukchi	15	own data
	4	Eskimos (Chukotka)	28	own data
	5	Aleuts	31	own data
	6	Buryats	228	archived data of N.N. Mamonova
	7	Kirghiz	21	own data
	8	Mongols	59	own data
	9	Khanty	99	own data
	10	Eskimos (Alaska)	111	Debets, 1986
	11	Yakuts	20	own data
		Total	786	

Macro-region	Nº	Ethno-territorial group	n	Source
Eastern Asia	12	Tibetans	47	Morant, 1924
	13	Nepalese	32	Morant, 1924
	14	Hokien	36	Harrower, 1924
	15	Taiyuan	69	Wang, Sun, 1988
	16	Japanese Hokuriku	30	Goro Shimabukuro, 1933 (In Chinese)
	17	Hailam Chinese	39	own data
	18	Peking-Chinesen	27	own data
	19	Kilung-Chinesen	47	own data
	20	Peking-Chinesen	86	own data
	21	Fukien Chinese	36	own data
	22	Peking-Chinesen	19	own data
	23	Koreaner	137	own data
	24	Fuschun-Chinesen	77	own data
	25	Kinai-Japaner	30	own data
	26	Dairen-Chinesen	20	own data
	27	Formosa-Chinesen	14	own data
		Total	79	

Macro-region	Nº	Ethno-territorial group	n	Source
Southeast Asia	28	Aeta Agta, or Dumagat	33	Bonin, 1931a
	29	Bantam	22	Bonin, 1931a
	30	Burmese	60	Tildesley, 1921
	31	Dayaks	41	Bonin, 1931a
	32	Jakarta	33	Bonin, 1931a
	33	Madura Island	15	Bonin, 1931a
	34	Tagalog	31	Bonin, 1931a
	35	Javanese (1)	35	Bonin, 1931a
	36	Javanese (2)	29	Bonin, 1931a
		Total	299	
South Asia	37	Andamans	22	Bonin, 1931a
	38	Tamils	35	Harrower G. 1924
		Total	57	
Oceania	39	New Britain	127	Bonin, 1936
	40	Easter Island	54	Bonin, 1931b
	41	North New Guinea	87	Hambly, 1940
	42	South New Guinea	38	Hambly, 1940
		Total	306	

Macro-region	Nº	Ethno-territorial group	n	Source
North America	43	Belle Glade Indians	17	Hrdlicka 1927
	44	San Francisco Bay Indians	31	Hrdlicka 1927
	45	Kentucky Indians	34	Hrdlicka 1927
	46	Cape Canaveral Indians	52	Hrdlicka 1940
	47	New Jersey Indians	12	Hrdlicka 1927
	48	San Nicolas Island Indians	11	Hrdlicka 1927
	49	Santa Cruz Indians	64	Hrdlicka 1927
	50	Santa Rosa Indians	20	Hrdlicka 1927
	51	Manhattan Island Indians	11	Hrdlicka 1927
	52	St. Johns River Indians	16	Hrdlicka 1940
	53	Santa Barbara County Indians	48	Hrdlicka 1927
	54	North Dakota Indians	13	Hrdlicka 1927
	55	Florida Indians	9	Hrdlicka 1940
	56	Massachusetts Indians	14	Hrdlicka 1927
	57	New York State Indians	19	Hrdlicka 1927
	58	Northwest New York state Iroquois	33	Hrdlicka 1927
		Total	404	

Methods

The study of Latin American populations was carried out accord-ing to 11 craniological features of the standard program (Broca 1875; Martin 1928; Debets 1935; Alekseev and Debets 1964). Six features are of the *cerebral region*: longitudinal diameter (M.1), transverse diameter (M.8), height (M.17), length of the base of the skull (M.5), the smallest forehead width (M.9), the largest fore-head width (M.10). Five features are of the *facial region*: the length of the base of the face (M.40), the upper height of the face (M.48), the zygomatic diameter (M.45), the width of the nose (M.54), the height of the nose (M.55). For easier interpretation, a sche-matic representation of craniometric features is shown in the Figure 1.

All data used were taken from the literature and of course many of the published works provide a larger amount of cranio-metric data with other features. However, some features were not analyzed by us due to the fact that one cannot be sure of the com-parability of measurement methods, for example, with the size of the eye sockets, which has an extremely high inter-research discrepancy.

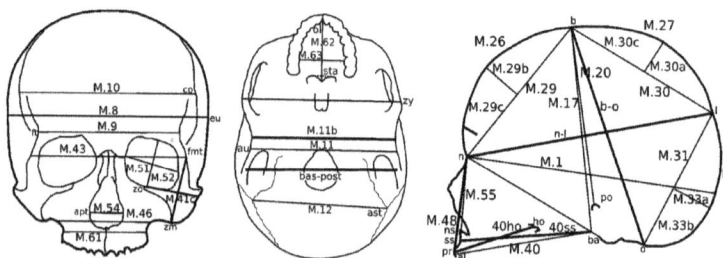

Figure 1. Schematic representation of craniometric features.

Results

Morphological description of South American groups

The first stage of the study was a morphological description of the groups from the territory of South America. It was made using categories of craniometric sizes. The categories were assigned according to the generally accepted craniometric constants which were calculated on the basis of the global variability in the size of the skull (Alekseev, Debets 1964). All feature values were assigned to one or another size category, from very small (1) to very large (5). For example, if the mean value of a certain feature of a group fell into the interval of very small values, it was assigned category 1. The values that fell into the interval of small values, 2, and so on up to very large values, which were assigned the value 5. Thanks to these categories, we can compare data for different groups more clearly, since there is some generalization of the data.

Only 4 out of 17 groups are characterized by a short (category 2) cerebral region of the skull (Figure 2). These are two groups from the territory of Peru (Calca and Chicama) and two from the territory of Chile (Mapuche and Araucano). Two more groups have a short brain region, on the border with a medium long one: a group from San Damian (Peru) and a group from the territory of Venezuela (lake Valencia). Four groups have long skulls (category 4), two from Patagonia and two from Tierra del Fuego, and the Ona series of Indians from Tierra del Fuego have a very long brain region (category 5). The remaining six groups, from the territories of Brazil, Argentina and Peru, have a medium-long braincase.

Almost all series (11 out of 17) have an average width of the brain region (Figure 3). Narrow skulls are characteristic of three series from the territory of Peru and of Botocudos from the territory of Brazil; the Lagoa Santa series from Brazil has a very narrow skull. The only series that is characterized by a wide brain region of the skull is the Patagonians of Rio Chubut.

The variation in skull height is more interesting (Figure 4). All the Patagonian skulls from the territory of Argentina have a very high or close to very high brain region. Four series are characterized by a high skull, all coming from different territories: Alakalufs (Tierra del Fuego), Paucarcancha (Peru), Araucans (Chile), and Botocudos (Brazil). Onas and Yagans from the territory of Tierra del Fuego have close to high values of the cerebral region height. The rest of the series from the territories of Peru, Chile, and Brazil are characterized by a medium-high cranial region, with the exception of the low skulls of the Indians of Venezuela and the Maqui-Maqui series from the territory of Peru. The geographic localization of low skulls in northern South America has been previously noted (Newman and Stewart 1950).

All series from Peru and Venezuela have a short cranial base (Figure 5). Groups from the territory of Brazil and Tierra del Fuego, as well as one group from the territory of Argentina, are characterized by a medium-long cranial base. And only two series from Argentina (Patagonians from Rio Chubut and Paraná) have a long skull base.

Interestingly, the forehead in the region of the postorbital constriction is narrow in most groups (Figure 6). a medium wide minimal forehead width can be found in some groups — all series from the territory of Argentina, as well as Araucanos from Chile, Maqui-Maqui from Peru and a series from the territory of Venezuela. High values of this feature are not observed. The same can be said about the width of the frontal bone in the region of the coronal suture (Figure 7). The Botocudos, the Lagoa Santa series, the Indians of Venezuela, the Patagonians of Argentina, and the Alakalufs from the territory of Tierra del Fuego have a very-narrow or narrow forehead. Five series, three from the territory of Tierra del Fuego and two from the territory of Chile, have a medium-wide forehead. For the groups from the territory of Peru, the size of the frontal bone at the coronal suture is unfortunately unknown.

The facial area of the Indian skulls from the territory of South America is quite variable in height (Figure 8). The skulls of the Peruvian series (with the exception of one), as well as the Lagoa Santa series, have a low face. Argentinean skulls and skulls of one of the Alakaluf series from Tierra del Fuego have a high facial region. The rest of the series are characterized by an average face height. Woefully, for the other series of Tierra del Fuego, as well as a series of Araucanian skulls, the height of the face is unknown.

The faces of South American Indians are generally wide or very wide (Figure 9), but there are six groups whose faces are of medium width. These are the Araucanians, the Lagoa Santa group and the four Peruvian series.

The nose is mostly medium wide (Figure 10), narrow only in three series from the territory of Peru.

The scatter is greater for the height of the nose (Figure 11). The Indians of Venezuela have a very high nose. The Indians of Tierra del Fuego and Argentina are characterized by a high nose. Most of the series from the territory of Peru, as well as the Lagoa Santa series, have a short nose. The four remaining series — ones from Brazil, Chile, Peru, and Argentina — are characterized by a medium high nose.

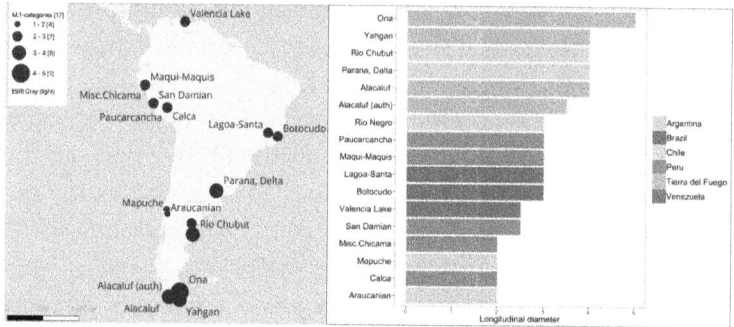

Figure 2. Categories of longitudinal diameter in different ethno-territorial groups.

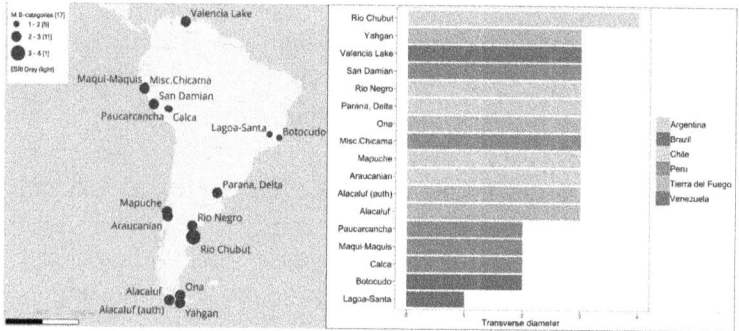

Figure 3. Categories of transverse diameter in different ethno-territorial groups.

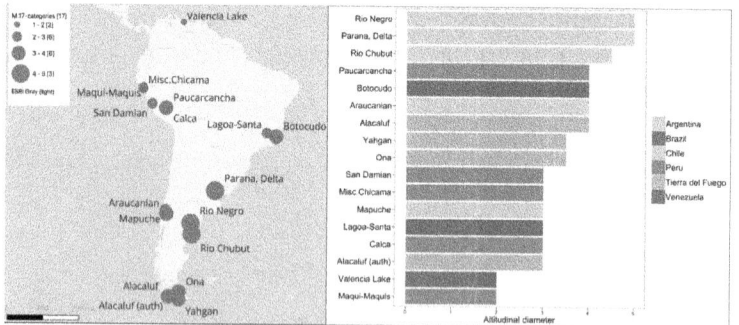

Figure 4. Categories of altitudinal diameter in different ethno-territorial groups.

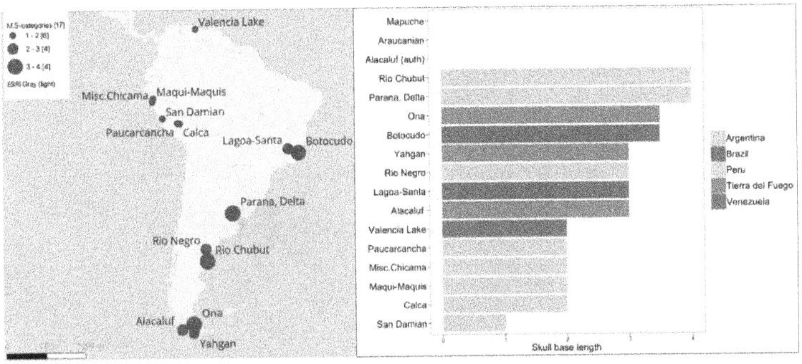

Figure 5. Categories of skull base length in different ethno-territorial groups.

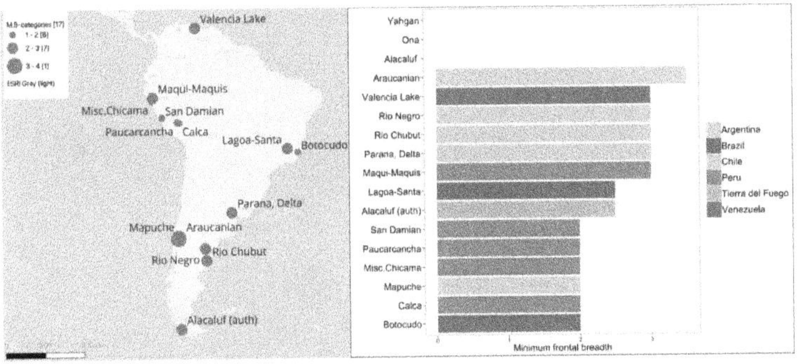

Figure 6. Categories of smallest forehead width (at the postorbital constriction) in different ethno-territorial groups.

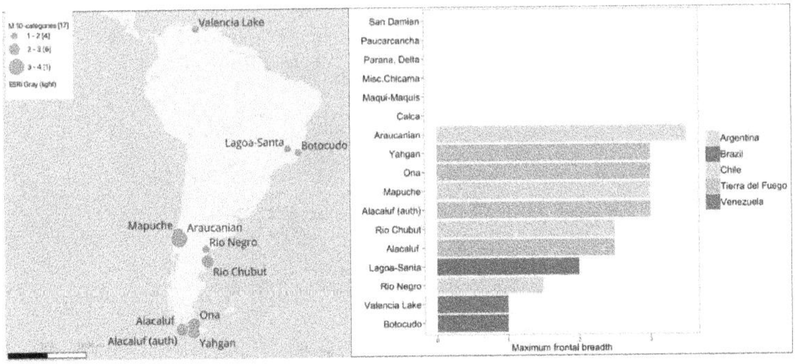

Figure 7. Categories of the width of the forehead at the coronal suture in different ethno-territorial groups.

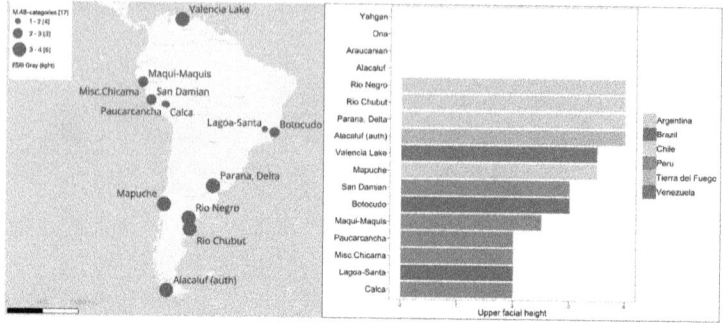

Figure 8. Categories of upper face height in different ethno-territorial groups.

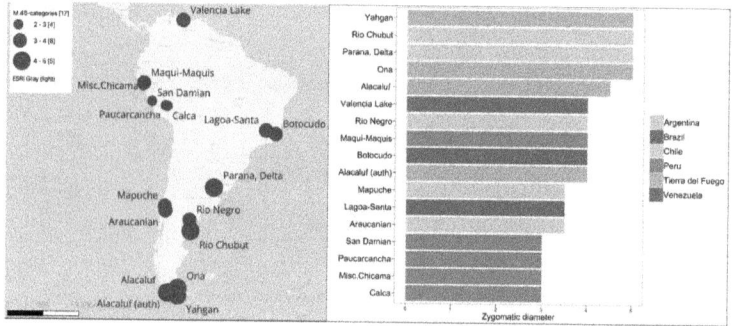

Figure 9. Categories of zygomatic diameter in different ethno-territorial groups.

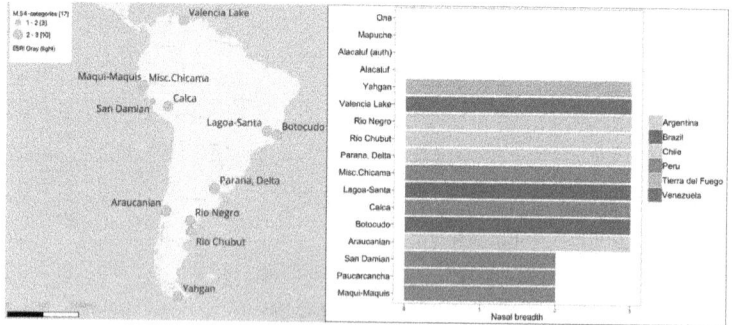

Figure 10. Categories of nose width in different ethno-territorial groups.

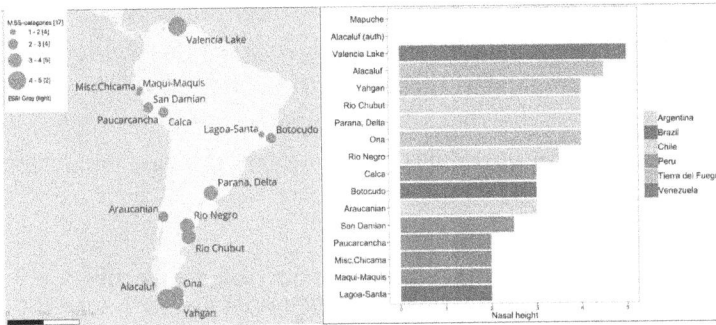

Figure 11. Categories of nose height in different ethno-territorial groups.

Intercontinental comparison

Multivariate analysis was carried out only on seven craniometric features: longitudinal, transverse and height diameters, upper face height, zygomatic diameter, nose height and width. Such a decrease in the number of features is associated with the mosaic nature of the initial data. Many groups, American as well as Asian, had a very limited set of features by which they were measured. We had to leave only those features that were present in all groups, since missing values cannot be analyzed in multivariate analyses. Several groups were also removed, for a total of 77 groups included in the analysis. For them, a canonical discriminant analysis was carried out by means, using general species constants (correlation coefficients and standard deviations). The differentiation of the groups turned out to be quite distinct (Figure 12). The division according to the first canonical vector was observed according to the features of the facial region: the height of the face, and the height and width of the nose (Table 3). in the area of high values, we have individuals with a high face and a wide and relatively short nose. in the second canonical vector, the transverse and height diameters of the brain region, as well as the height of the nose, turned out to be

29

significant. in the area of high values, there are individuals with a low and wide skull, and with a narrow nose. From the data presented, it can be noted that an unusual intergroup correlation is observed. Face height and nose height are negatively correlated, although their biological correlation in human populations is high and positive.

Table 3. Standardized coefficients of discriminant functions obtained as a result of canonical discriminant analysis by means.

Cranial Features	1st canonical vector	2nd canonical vector
% Variation Explained	53,898	18,57
Longitudinal diameter M.1	-0.16	0.18
Transverse diameter M.8	0.42	-0.71
Height diameter M.17	-0.22	0.64
Upper face height M.48	0.84	0.52
Cheekbone diameter M.45	0.04	0.28
Nose height M.55	-0.74	-0.76
Nose width M.54	0.71	0.13

In the left area of the graph groups from the territory of Australia and Oceania are located. On the opposite side, rather scattered, are groups from the territory of North Asia. Thus, we observe a separation according to the height of the face and the width of the nose. Groups from other regions were distributed among them. The groups of East Asia are close to the generality of North America, which is consistent with the results of previous studies. At the same time, it can be seen from the distribution plot that the area occupied by the North American series includes almost completely the area occupied by the

East Asian groups. At the same time, the area occupied by the groups of North Asia is the most extensive and is shifted from the other two in the direction of increasing the height of the face and the width of the nose, and some heterogeneity in the second canonical vector can be seen. The Southeast Asian groups are as compact as the East Asian groups. They ended up at the bottom of the graph, with relatively high noses and a low and wide skull.

Nearby (in the upper part of the distribution) are the series from the territory of Argentina, as well as Botocudos from the territory of Brazil. The Peruvian series are located at the bottom of the distribution, closer to the Southeast Asia and Oceania series. The Lagoa Santa group is in the area of distribution of the groups from the territory of Australia and Oceania, closest to the series from the territory of Easter Island and the Torres Islands. It is believed that this series is rather ancient. This location in the graph may indicate that the ancient population of America had a connection with the populations of Australia and Oceania. The series from the territory of Venezuela stands out from the general distribution, being close to the series of the Mongols from the territory of Central Asia.

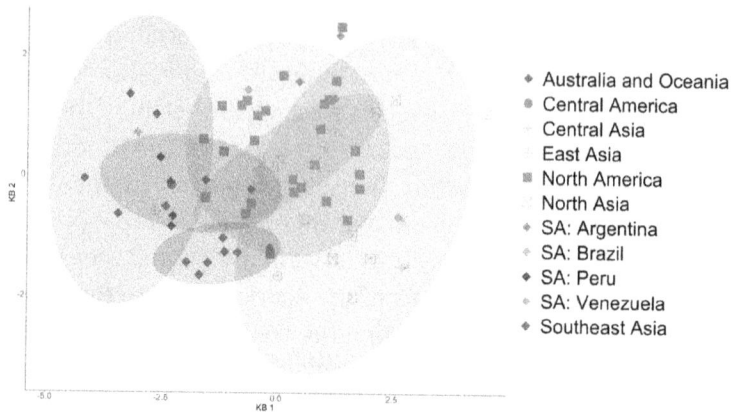

* Australia and Oceania
* Central America
  Central Asia
  East Asia
* North America
  North Asia
* SA: Argentina
* SA: Brazil
* SA: Peru
* SA: Venezuela
* Southeast Asia

a)

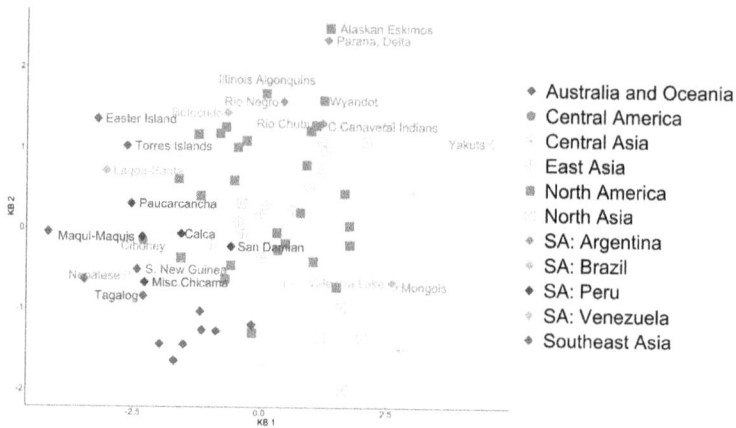

* Australia and Oceania
* Central America
  Central Asia
  East Asia
* North America
  North Asia
* SA: Argentina
* SA: Brazil
* SA: Peru
* SA: Venezuela
* Southeast Asia

b)

Figure 12. a) the distribution of groups in the space of the first and second canonical vectors with ellipses representing the 90% confidence interval; b) the distribution of groups in the space of the first and second canonical vectors, on which the South American series and series close to them from other territories are indicated.

Conclusion

Taking into account everything abovementioned, it can be concluded that some heterogeneity can be observed on the territory of South America. Even in this mosaic material, it is clear that there are skulls with larger sizes of the brain region and those that have smaller sizes. The first group includes one series from the territory of Argentina based on some features, and one from the territory of Brazil — both from the east coast. On the other hand, small sizes of the brain section can be found in series of the north and northeast: Peru, Venezuela. We notice as well a north-south increase in the forehead width. The overall dimensions of the face also increase from north to south.

At the same time, multivariate analysis shows that the groups from the territory of Peru are isolated. a series of Parana stands out, approaching the Eskimos of Alaska (Figure 12). The Patagonians and Botocudos from the east coast are isolated as well. The series from the territory of Venezuela is also separated from other South American series, towards the groups of Central and North Asia.

Of course, such disparate data include many unpredictable factors that affect the results, starting with the fact that the features could be measured differently by different authors and ending with the fact that some series may include skulls with artificial deformation or be of very different antiquity. All this does not allow us to draw final conclusions. It is necessary to re-collect data, as well as to study other groups from these territories, which could describe in more detail the morphological variability of the indigenous population of Latin America.

References

Alekseev, Debets 1964 — Alekseev V.P., Debets G.F. Kraniometriya. Metodika antropologicheskikh issledovaniy [Craniometry. Methods of anthropological research]. Moscow: Nauka, 1964. (In Russ.)

Debets 1935 — Debets G.F. K unifikatsii kraniologicheskikh issledovaniy [Towards the unification of craniological research] // Antropologicheskiy zhurnal [Anthropological journal]. 1935. V.1. P. 118-124. (In Russ.)

Debets 1986 — Debets G.F. Paleoantropologiya drevnih eskimosov (Ipiutak, Tigara) [Paleoanthropology of ancient Eskimos (Ipiutak, Tigara)] // Etnicheskie svyazi narodov severa Azii i Ameriki po dannym antropologii [Ethnic relations of the peoples of the North of Asia and America]. Moscow: Nauka, 1986. P. 6–149. (In Russ.).

Bonin 1931a — Bonin G. von. Beitrag Zur Kraniologie von Ost-Asien // Biometrika. 1931. 23 (1/2). P. 52–113.

Bonin 1931b — Bonin G. von. a Contribution to the Craniology of the Easter Islanders // Biometrika. 1931. 23 (3/4). P. 249–270.

Bonin 1936 — Bonin G. von. on the Craniology of Oceania. Crania from New Britain // Biometrika. 1936. 28 (1/2). P. 123–148.

Broca 1875 — Broca P. Instructions craniologiques et craniometriques. Memoires d. Paris, 1875.

Ehrenreich 1887 — Ehrenreich P. Espiritu Ueber die Botocudos der brasilianischen Provinzen santo und Minas Geraes // Zeitschrift Für Ethnologie. 1887. Vol. 19. P. 49–82.

Ericksen 1962 — Ericksen M.F. Undeformed pre-Columbian crania from the North Sierra of Peru // American Journal of Physical Anthropology. 1962. Vol. 20(2). P. 209-222.

Goro Shimabukuro 1933 — Goro Shimabukuro. Anthropological study of Chinese skulls in rural Fushun (first report) // Journal of Anthropology. 1933. Vol. 48(8). P. 423-537. (in Chinese)

Hambly 1940 — Hambly W.D. Craniometry of New Guinea. Chicago, 1940.

Harrower 1924 — Harrower G.A. Study of the Hokien and Tamil Skull. Biometrika, 1924.

Hernández et al. 1997 — Hernández M., Fox C.L., García-Moro C. Fueguian cranial morphology: the adaptation to a cold, harsh environment // American Journal of Physical Anthropology. 1997. Vol. 103(1). P. 103-17.

Howells 1940—Howells W.W. The Origin of American Indian Race Types // the Maya and their Neighbours. N.Y., 1940.

Hrdlicka 1911—Hrdlicka A. Some results of recent anthropological exploration in Peru // Smithsonian Misc. Coll. Vol. 56 no. 16.

Hrdlicka 1914—Hrdlicka A. Anthropological work in Peru in 1913, with notes on the pathology of the ancient Peruvians // Smithsonian Misc. Coll. Vol. 61 no. 18.

Hrdlička 1927—Hrdlička A. Catalogue of human crania in the United States National Museum collections: the Algonkin and related Iroquois; Sinuan, Caddoan, Salish and Sahaptin, Shoshonean, and Californian Indians // Proceedings of the United States National Museum. Vol. 69 no. 2631. P. 1–127.

Hrdlička 1940—Hrdlička, A. Catalog of human crania in the United States National Museum collections: Indians of the Gulf States // Proceedings of the United States National Museum. Vol. 87 no. 3076. P. 315–464.

Ismagulov 1970—Ismagulov O. Naselenie Kazakhstana ot ehpokhi bronzy do sovremennosti (paleoantropologicheskoe issledovanie) [The population of Kazakhstan from the Bronze Age to the present (paleoanthropological study)]. Alma-Ata: Nauka, 1970. (In Russ.)

Latcham 1904—Latcham R.E. Notes on the Physical Characteristics of the Araucanos // J. Anthropol. Inst. of GB and Ireland. 1904. Vol. 34. P. 170-180.

MacCurdy 1923—MacCurdy, G.G. Human skeletal remains from the highlands of Peru // Am. J. Phys. Anthrop. 1923. Vol. 6. P. 217-329.

Marelli 1913—Marelli C.A. Contribución a la craneología de las primitivas poblaciones de la Patagonia (observaciones morfobiométricas) // Anales del Museo nacional de historia natural de Buenos Aires. 1913. T. XXVI. P. 31-91.

Martin 1896—Martin R. Altpatagonitche Schadel // Vierteljahrsschrift der Naturforschenden Gesellschaft in Zürich. 1896. Vol. 41.

Martin 1928—Martin R. Lehrbuch der Anthropologie. 2-te Aufl. Bd. II, 1928.

Morant 1924—Morant G.M. a Study of Certain Oriental Series of Crania Including the Nepalese and Tibetan Series in the British Museum (Natural History) // Biometrika. 1924. 16 (1/2). P. 1–10.

Neves, Hubbe 2005—Neves W.A., Hubbe M. Cranial morphology of early Americans from Lagoa Santa, Brazil: Implications for the settlement of the New World // PNAS. 2005. Vol. 102 (51). P. 18309-18314.

35

Neves et al. 2007—Neves W.A., Hubbe M., Correal G. Human Skeletal Remains from Sabana de Bogota, Colombia: a Case of Paleoamerican Morphology Late Survival in South America? // Am. J. Phys. Anthrop. 2007. Vol. 133. P. 1080–1098.

Newman 1943—Newman M.T. a metric study of undeformed Indian crania from Peru // Am. J. Phys. Anthrop. 1943. Vol. 1 issue 1. P. 21-45.

Newman 1962—Newman M.T. Evolutionary Changes in Body Size and Head Form in American Indians // American Anthropologist, New Series. 1962. Vol. 64 no. 2. P. 237-257.

Newman, Stewart 1950—Newman, M.T., Stewart T.D. Skeletal remains of South American Indians // J.H. Steward (ed.). Handbook of South American Indians. Vol. 6. Physical Anthropology, Linguistics, and Cultural Geography of South American Indians. Washington, DC: US Government Printing Office, 1950. P. 19-42.

Pestryakov, Grigorieva 2009—Pestryakov A.P., Grigorieva O.M. Kraniologiya avtokhtonnogo naseleniya i problema pervonachal'nogo zaseleniya Ameriki [Craniology of the autochthonous population and the problem of the initial settlement of America] // Vestnik antropologii [Bulletin of Anthropology]. 2009. No. 17. P. 211-223.

Rey 1880—Rey P.M. Étude anthropologique sur les Botocudos. Paris: Octave Doin, 1880.

Rivet 1908—Rivet P. La Race de Lagoa-Santa chez les populations précolombiennes de l'Equateur // Bulletins et Mémoires de la Société d'anthropologie de Paris. 1908. Vol. 9 no. 1. P. 209-274.

Rodrigues Peixoto 1885—Rodrigues Peixoto J. Novos estudos craniológicos sobre os Botocudos // Archiv. Mus. Nac. Rio de Janeiro. 1885. Vol. 6. P. 205-256.

Rodríguez 2007—Rodríguez C. J.V. La diversidad poblacional de Colombia en el tiempo y el espacio: Estudio craneométrico cranial variation of the colombian prehispanic populations // Rev. Acad. Colomb. Cienc. 2007. Vol. 31 (120). P. 321-346.

Rodríguez 1987—Rodríguez C. J.V. Algunos aspectos metodológico-bioantropológicos relacionados con el poblamiento de América. Maguaré, 1987.

Roginsky 1937—Roginsky Y.Y. Problema proiskhozhdeniya mongol'skogo rasovogo tipa [The problem of the origin of the Mongolian racial type] //

Antropologicheskiy zhurnal [Anthropological journal]. 1937. No. 2. P. 43-63. (In Russ.)

Stewart 1943—Stewart T.D. Skeletal remains with cultural associations from the Chicama, Moche, and Virii Valleys, Peru // Proc. U. S. Nat. Mus. 1943. Vol. 93. P. 153-185.

Tildesley 1921—Tildesley M.L. a First Study of the Burmese Skull // Biometrika. 1921. Vol. 13 (2/3). P. 176–262.

Wang, Sun 1988—Wang L., Sun F. a study on the skulls from Taiyuan, Shanxi // Acta Anthropologica Sinica. 1988. Vol. 7 (03). P. 206-214.

Zamakona de Arechavaleta, Lagrange de Castillo 2007—Zamakona de Arechavaleta G., Lagrange de Castillo H. Craneología indígena de Venezuela. Cráneos no deformados y deformados. La Pica, Estado Aragua, Venezuela // Revista de la Sociedad Venezolana de Historia de la Medicina. 2007. Vol. 56, no. 1-2.

Zubov 1999—Zubov A.A. Biologo-antropologicheskaya kharakteristika korennogo doyevropeyskogo naseleniya Ameriki [Biological and anthropological characteristics of the indigenous pre-European population of America] // Istomin A.A. (ed.). Naseleniye Novogo Sveta: Problemy formirovaniya I sotsiokulturnogo razvitiya [Population of the New World: Problems of Formation and Socio-Cultural Evolution]. Moscow: Nauka, 1999. P. 42-43. (In Russ.)

Concept of Soul
in the Andean Worldview

Elena V. Novoselova

Introduction

The concept of soul is universal and typical for most models of the worldview. However, it often happens that within the same tradition there are some variations of its embodiment. The Andean worldview can serve as an example of such development. From a historical point of view, the concept of soul is one of the most difficult to study in the entire ideological complex of the Andean cultures. First of all, this is due to the lack of reliable narrative sources for the most period of the independent development of the Andean civilization, in other words, before the arrival of Europeans and before the Spanish conquest. However, the complex use of available sources (written evidence of the early colonial period of various types and genres, archaeological sites — especially burials, — ethnographic data and iconography) allows us to make some observations about the theme and come to certain conclusions.

Before the analysis itself, we would like to emphasize that authentic narrative sources are extremely important for understanding this concept. Only such sources can give clear explanations and interpretations of various traditions and beliefs related to the idea of the soul. But in the case of the Andean civilization, we do not have such sources, and, as a result, the data on the concept of soul that we have are only fragments of a once vast complex of beliefs. Eventually many provisions can be established only indirectly, based on comparative materials.

It should also be noted that the concept of soul is closely related to the ideas of afterlife and a journey after death. Moreover, the most important data about the concept of soul in the Andes refer to this very specific context. These data are usually quite late and related to ethnographic observations mainly in the 20th and 21th centuries.

The historiography of the topic is very numerous, however, it is rather fragmentary in terms of the concept of soul, since it is most often analyzed not independently, but as part of more extensive ideological complexes. It is necessary to mention some studies devoted to the modern Andean worldview that touch upon the idea of soul (Arguedas 1953; Carter 1968; van den Berg 1989; van Kessel 2001; Bascopé Caero 2001; Vaderrana Fernández, Escalante Gutierrez 1980; Fernández Juárez 2001; Lefranc 2015).

First of all, it is important to analyze the terminological aspect of the problem, at least in general terms. in the written sources, the most common terms for the soul are *alma, ánima,* and *coraje*. The first two words can be preponderated directly as "soul", the third one has the meaning "courage, bravery". It is significant that these terms have Spanish origins and were borrowed by Native American languages such as Quechua and Aymara. This clearly indicates that the Christian concept of soul conveyed by these terms was alien to the Andean worldview, otherwise there would be no need to borrow the words. in the case of Native American languages, it is well known that Spanish terms necessary for an adequate expression of the basic concepts of Christianity were borrowed among the first (Dedenbach-Salazar 2003: 391). The concept of soul, of course, belonged to such borrows.

In addition to the terms mentioned above, there are a number of other words of a more local significance, some of which will be discussed below. Here we note that among them there are words of both Spanish and Indian origin that reflect the mixture of ideological concepts and the syncretic nature of the concept of soul at the present stage of the Andean worldview.

The sources, with all their fragmentary nature, allow us to distinguish the following features of the Andean concept of soul: 1) the idea of multiplicity of souls; 2) materiality of soul; 3) metaphorical image of soul; 4) close involvement of souls in the general cycle of birth and death. We will analyze each of these aspects in more detail below.

The idea of plurality of souls

The idea that a person has several souls at once is quite contradictory in the Andes. On the one hand, there are no mentions of this idea in the written narrative sources of the colonial era, which reflect the state of the Andean worldview, close to the "original» one. But such mentions are quite common in ethnographic sources, and we will talk about it in more detail below.

It is necessary to mention some typical features of the colonial sources in the context of the theme. As a rule, these sources are dedicated to the Inca state or the beliefs of indigenous peoples of the colonial era and pay little attention to the concept of soul. Obviously, it is a consequence of the influence of the Christian worldview characterized by the idea of a single soul. But it is clear that the concepts of multiple souls are very common in different cultures and in various regions of our planet. Moreover, in general we can say that the concept of a single soul is more typical for revealed religions, while for polytheistic ones such concept is not common. For this reason, it can be thought that the colonial written sources do not fully reflect the features of the Andean concept of soul, rather, they represent its simplified version, which is closest to the features of the European worldview and the European concept of soul. This is in good agreement with the general ideas about chronicles as sources, in most of which the Andean worldview is understood quite schematically and sometimes frankly wrong.

Here are some quotes from the chronicles that deal with the soul: "Comúnmente creyeron que las ánimas vivían después de esta vida y que los buenos tenían gloria y los malos pena" (Ondegardo 1906, 208); "el ánima, y le ofrecen, derramando mucho vino, y a la mañana dicen que ya está el ánima en Zamay huaci, que quiere decir casa del descanso, y que no volverá más" (Arriaga 1999, 66). As we can see, the idea of multiplicity of soul is not mentioned in these citations, and the analyzed concept of soul is presented in a Christian way. As an analogy, we can cite numerous cases of describing the soul among the peoples of Siberia and the Far East: they were also characterized by the ideas of multiplicity of souls, but the first researchers of these worldviews tried to describe this concept using Christian terminology, which only obscured the meaning of the original ideas. a similar situation can be observed in the Andes.

At the same time, it should be emphasized that modern ethnographic sources on the Andean worldview confirm the existence of the idea of plurality of souls. We can give some examples from different regions of the Andes. This list does not pretend to be exhaustive, but even it shows a wide variety of relevant representations. in the Bolivian Altiplano, different informants gave various information about the number of souls: four (*ajar, janayu, coraje, ánima*) or even five (*ajayu, ánima, janayu, amasa, coraje*), but the first one is considered as the most important

(Carter 1968: 246–247). We should also pay attention to the fact that the most complete picture of souls was given by an old soothsayer. Unfortunately, the publication does not provide precise information about what exactly is the difference between these souls (in addition to the gradation of their importance) and what is their posthumous fate. in relatively new ethnological data (the beginning of the 21ᵗʰ century) from the same region, we have some notions about three souls: *ajayu, animu, kuraji*. *Ajayu* is still considered as the most important soul, and its loss threatens with almost inevitable death (Alvarado 2019: 97). It is not difficult to notice that the names of less important souls are borrowed from the Spanish language, while the original word is used to designate the main one.

At the same time, in other Andean regions, Apurimac and Tarapaca, there was documented a belief in the existence of two and three souls. in the first case, they are called *alma major* and *alma menor*. At first, they exist separately from each other, but after they must unite and go to the Underworld together. However, it often does not happen, and *alma menor* remains in this world where it can harm the living (Valderrana, Escalante 1980: 240). in the second case (in Tarapak), three souls have three different paths after death: the first goes to heaven, the second stays with relatives for at least a year, and the third stays near the grave for two years (Ortega 2001: 254). Again, it is unclear what happens to them after the designated period. Among the laymis of Bolivia, there is also a fixed idea of three souls one of which goes to the heaven and the others, to the "Andean" Underworld, which is situated either across the sea or in the bowels of the mountain (Harris 1983: 145-146). So, we can say that these ideas are quite contradictory and fragmentary in some aspects.

Also worth mentioning is the idea of different destinies of souls depending on the age and other factors. There are also many variations in this aspect, but the special status of children's souls, which are called *angélitos* («little angels»), is almost universal. The attitude towards them is purely positive; it is believed that they can positively influence on various aspects of everyday life, for example the weather. Only two sources mention that only baptized children have this status (van Kessel 2001: 221; Fernandez 2001: 205), while unbaptized ones go to snow-covered mountain peaks, where they can influence on the weather. Most often it is about children in general (van der Berg 1989: 157; Ortega 2001: 257; Bascopé Caero 2001: 275).

Judging by the fact that the concept of *angélitos* is found in the fiction of the 19ᵗʰ century already in fully developed form*, it appeared even earlier. The idea of the special status of children is twofold. On the one hand, the idea that children, regardless of baptism, receive privileges in the Underworld, can be seen as contrary to the Christian concept. On the other hand, the traditional Andean worldview, as far as it can be judged, basically had no idea of any afterlife preferences: in the afterlife, everyone continued to lead the same life as on the Earth. Apparently, here we have an example of the development of an idea that is a fusion of traditional and Christian ideas and cannot be unambiguously reduced to one prototype. We note also that a similar concept of *angélitos* is observed in some areas of Mexico (Strupp Green 1980: 57).

Another category of persons whose posthumous fate differs from the bulk of the population is the so-called *condenados*. This word can be translated as "sinners", and usually they were really guilty of serious crimes (for example, murder, suicide, theft) (van Kessel 2001: 222). However, sometimes souls become *condenados*

---

* in Ricardo Palma's «Cien tradiciones peruanas» it is reported that there is no need for the services of mourners at the funeral of children, because the souls of children (which are also called *angélitos* here) get to heaven without difficulty (Palma 1977, 183). It is interesting to compare a new aspect of the worldview with the old one: the tradition of mourning the deceased with loud sobs on the part of women goes back to the pre-Hispanic era (Cobo 1893, 236-237; Pizarro 2013; Cieza de León 2005, 78 53, 121).

not because of their own sins, but because of the tragic circumstances of death or out of revenge (Arguedas 1953: 135–138;
Lefranc 2015: 173–174). Most often, these *condenados* threaten
travelers, lying in wait for them on the roads and devouring them
(van Kessel 2001: 221), while they differ in a repulsive appearance. in his "Cuentos mágico-realistas", José María Arguedas
cites many stories related to *condenados*: it is obvious from them
that these souls pose the greatest threat to children and drunks.
The motive of the road as a dangerous place is also important.
It is very universal and cannot be unambiguously attributed either to the pre-Hispanic or to the Christian worldview.

At first glance, the *condenado* motif illustrates the influence of Christian ideas, according to which sinners are pun-
ished in the afterlife. However, it is not so clear. There are reasons to suppose that many ideas of pre-Christian origin have
been preserved in these concepts. This is especially true of souls
turned into *condenados* not because of their own sins, but because of external circumstances. Here is an example from a story about a man who became a *condenado* after a tragic death
in a mine. Returning home, he ate his three daughters, and when
he was burned, the souls of these girls went to the heaven in the
form of three white doves (Arguedas 1953: 139). The latter circumstance clearly echoes the ideas about *angélitos*, but here we
would like to draw attention to something else. This man turned
into a *condenado* not through his own fault, but because of the
circumstances of his death, which is completely inconsistent
with the Christian idea of retribution. in Christianity, there is an
idea of a "good" (expected, calm death in the family circle) and
a "bad" (violent, sudden) death, but not in such an exaggerated
form: a "bad" death is a possible, but it is not an obligatory reason
for the transformation of the soul into a restless spirit. in addition, the idea of turning such souls into cruel cannibals also has
no indisputable prototypes in Christianity. in this regard, it can

be assumed that the roots of ideas about *condenados* should be sought in the pre-Hispanic era.

Of course, the list of examples given regarding the number of souls can be expanded, and in this respect, we do not pretend to be complete. But already on their basis, we can formulate some observations. First of all, it is obvious that this aspect of the Andean worldview cannot be brought to a common denominator, since its manifestations are too diverse. Secondly, in this case, social and age stratification and differentiation are very indicative, especially in the case of people associated with the cult and rituals. in other words, it is obvious that such people have a more detailed and elaborated image of the soul, while younger people have a simpler and more schematic view on this concept. This information is also very useful for analyzing the current state of the Andean worldview in general.

As a result, we can say that it is unlikely that all these ideas analyzed above have appeared recently. It is more likely that they have a rather ancient origin. Most likely they are fragments of pre-Christian and pre-Hispanic ideas about the soul. But unfortunately, it is impossible to say which representations were more typical for different regions of the Andes in the pre-Hispanic period. Given the diversity and variability of the picture of the Andean worldview, it is logical to assume that the idea of the multiplicity of the soul was represented by a large number of regional variants.

The idea of materiality of soul

Another important motive of the concept of soul in the Andean worldview is the fact that souls were considered a substance closely related to matter. In other words, the soul was perceived as something material. Such ideas are closely related to its posthumous fate. There are many descriptions in written sources that help us prove this observation. As an example, we can cite one mention from the text by Polo de Ondegardo about the rituals and ceremonies of the Indigenous people. The value of this source is enhanced by the fact that it is quite early. It says: "Creen también que las ánimas de los difuntos andan vagas y solitarias por este mundo padeciendo hambre, sed, frío, calor y cansancio" ("They also believe that the souls of the dead wander alone in this world, suffering from hunger, thirst, heat and fatigue") (Ondegardo 1906: 196). Another example from Martín de Murúa's chronicle, *the Universal History of Peru*, repeats almost verbatim the previous passage: "Tenían otro error, que las ánimas andaban vagas y solitarias y padecían hambre, sed, y frío y cansancio" (Murúa 2001: 403). Antonio de la Calancha repeats Ondegardo's description almost completely (Calancha 1638: 377). Based on the quotes cited above, it can be concluded that the definition of Murúa and Calancha was borrowed from Ondegardo's text.

In any case, according to these chroniclers, souls can feel hunger, cold, etc., in other words, the carriers of the Andean worldview perceive them as material substances. We can analyze numerous rituals from funerary contexts according to this idea. Relevant archaeological data is huge, so here we will limit ourselves to general remarks that directly relate to the concept of soul. First of all, we should mention the custom of putting food, drinks, vessels, clothes, etc. in graves. It is practically a common place for the entire period of the existence of the Andean civilization, from the earliest cultures to the present. Of course, there is a lot of variability in terms of place, time, etc., but this does not detract from the universality of the custom. It is significant that such offerings are found in the graves of persons of different social status, which clearly shows not only the social, but also the ideological function of these rituals. In this case, we see a kind of desire to protect with offerings the soul from various sufferings that may happen to it on the way to the Underworld. This interpretation is confirmed by modern ethnographic data, since the inhabitants of the Andes directly testify to this function of offerings (Bascopé Caero 2001: 273; Luperio 2001: 238). They believe that food and *chicha* can help their deceased relatives get into the Underworld. With the recently deceased, offerings can also be given to previously deceased relatives (Carter 1968: 243). If the soul was a purely spiritual substance, there would be no need for this.

Thus, the Andean concept of soul is closely connected with the body in which it lived, and retains many of its features. in this regard, the following fact is indicative: during the struggle against idolatry among the indigenous, they explained their unwillingness to bury the dead according to the Christian rite by the fact that the earth "presses" on the deceased (Arriaga 1999: 67). It is also significant that even in modern language, the word *alma* sometimes means not the soul, but the body of the deceased (Spedding 2008: 86) or his bones (Ortega 2001: 254). a rather archaic character of such ideas is evidenced by the lack of abstraction and distancing of the soul from the body. It is obvious that they have very ancient roots and go back to the early stages of the development of the Andean worldview.

Perhaps the idea of the materiality of the soul is connected (at least in part) with the tradition of preserving bodies or mummification in many Andean cultures. Maybe one of the souls was thought of as being in the body of the deceased, while the other/ others went to the Underworld. Although at a late stage in the development of Andean cultures, different types of communication with the bodies of deceased ancestors had an important political function (its culmination was the ceremonial treatment of imperial Inca mummies), it was undoubtedly secondary to the ritual function. It is impossible to confirm this hypothesis for certain due to the lack of suitable written sources*, however, the idea

* in a small treatise *Costumbres antiguas del Perú*, there is a rather vague indication of the Inca belief that the souls of the dead return to their bodies after some time and

that one of the souls continues to be in the body or at the burial place is quite typical for worldviews with concepts of plurality of souls (similar ideas in the Andes were discussed above). Be that as it may, the idea of a close connection between the incorruptible body and the posthumous fate of the soul is obvious, even if the nature of this connection is unknown to us exactly. It is also obvious that the transformation of the funeral rites under the influence of the Christianity had a strong impact on the Andean concept of soul in the direction of reducing its materiality and weakening the close connection between the body of the deceased and his soul/souls.

It is known that the very idea of the soul's needs for material goods was condemned by the Church, and the ideas of hunger, thirst, etc., which the soul allegedly experiences, are understood in the materials of the Lima Church councils (Ugarte 1951: 29, 253). This is not surprising, because in the Christianity, the only thing the soul needs after death is prayers, and not material goods in the form of food or clothing. Whatever it was, the corresponding rituals turned out to be very tenacious in the Andes and continue to function at least partially. Consequently, the ideas on which these rituals are based are also alive, even if not in their original form.

The modern Quechuan folklore also reflects ideas about the quite material nature of the soul. in particular, one of the fairy tales talks about a man who saw that his dead wife suddenly resurrected. She was dressed in the same clothes in which she had been buried, and after her resurrection she did the same daily work as during her lifetime (Payne 2000: 78). Or another example, even more revealing: a beautiful young man appeared to the girl at night, with whom, judging by the context, she entered into a love affair, but in the light of the sun he turned into

resurrect (Valera 1956: 18). However, it is difficult to draw far-reaching conclusions only on its basis; Christian influence is not excluded here either.

a skeleton (Payne 2000: 90–92). It is obvious that the girl took the young man for a living person. in this case, the materiality of the spirit is beyond doubt*. The following circumstance is also curious: he is called the spirit of an ancient ancestor, that is, the spirit of pre-Christian times. They are often referred to by the term *gentiles* (Fuenzalida 1977: 64-65), that is, "pagans", which confirms their status. in some Andean areas, these spirits are associated with the Inca era (Vilcapoma 2015, 27). At the same time, the term *alma* is never used in relation to non-Christian ancestors (Meconi 1990: 151–152).

Ethnographic studies note that these souls are often hostile to their distant descendants living at the present time, in particular, becoming the causes of epidemics (van Kessel 2001: 222; Spedding 2008, 74; Rivet, Tomasi 2016: 391–392). in our opinion, this is undoubted evidence of a clear gap in the cultural and ideological continuity between the pre-Hispanic period and the present. Moreover, the cave (Arguedas 1953: 149, 139, 169) often acts as a haven for such spirits — a place closely connected with the dead and the afterlife of the pre-Christian era, which will be discussed in more detail below.

The idea of metaphoricity of soul

On the other hand, the Andean idea of the soul was not only material, but also metaphorical. The metaphoricity can be understood as a stable connection of the soul with certain objects which are represented both with its symbols and material embodiments. in particular, the most common metaphor for the soul in the Andes is fly. Especially interesting is the fact that we can find such metaphors in pre-Hispanic sources. The most famous and early

* of course, all these mentions cannot do without some inconsistency. Thus, in one of the stories it is reported that when *condenado* is eating, food falls to the floor (Arguedas 1953, 147), that is, his body is too ephemeral to hold food.

example is the iconography of the Moche culture, where images of funerals or the afterlife scenes are accompanied by images of flies or similar small insects (Hocquenghem 1989: 94–95). We can also find a comparison of souls and flies in colonial sources, for example, in *Dioses y hombres* by Huarochiri: "En los tiempos muy antiguos, cuando un hombre moría, dejaban su cadáver, así nomás, tal como había muerto, durante cinco días. Al término de este plazo se desprendía su ánima ¡sí!, diciendo, como si fuera una mosca pequeña" (Arguedas 2015: 155). There are quite numerous mentions of flies in modern ethnographic materials (see below). This testifies to the stability of the corresponding ideas over a long period of existence of the Andean civilization. Perhaps this idea is related to the concept of a multiple soul, otherwise the journey to the Underworld would not have seemed so difficult. in other words, one of the souls could have the appearance of an insect, and the other (making a difficult journey to the next world) was thought to be anthropomorphic. Unfortunately, we cannot reliably confirm this hypothesis.

It should be noted that in the modern Andean worldview, the concept of the insect soul has acquired a metaphorical character in the narrow sense of the word. in other words, a fly or another insect often acts as a symbol of the soul, rather than its direct embodiment. This is indicated by signs according to which the appearance of insects portends someone's death or simply indicate the arrival of the soul during the feast of All Saints (Bascopé Caero 2001: 275; Luperio 2001: 236). in this case, insects act as symbols of death, and not personifications of someone's specific souls. However, in some places there is also a more traditional perception of the concept of the insect soul. in this case, flies during the *Todos los santos* day are perceived as the souls of the dead who have flown to see relatives and taste treats prepared especially for them (van der Berg 1989: 161; Valderrana, Escalante 1980: 264).

The idea of soul as a component of vital cycle

Finally, we have designated the last aspect of the Andean concept of soul as "close involvement of the soul in the general cycle
of birth and death." This aspect will allow us to directly approach
the understanding of what the soul is within the framework
of the traditional Andean worldview.

Speaking about the great involvement of the soul in the cycle
of birth and death, first of all we mean the following circumstance. Some sources of the colonial period recorded in a number
of regions of the Sierra contain ideas about the so-called *pacarina*, that is, the source from where the life comes and where souls
return after death. It is noteworthy that the semantics of the word
itself is associated with the birth, not death (Arriaga 1999: 74).
Most of the references come from documents on extirpation
of idolatries, but they are also found in chronicles, for example,
in Fernando de Santillan's one: "Todos creían [...] que el que era
bueno, cuando moría volvía a donde había venido, que era debajo
de la tierra, y que allí vivían los hombres y tenía todo descanso" (Santillan 1879: 35). The place itself is not named here, but
it is undoubtedly a *pacarina*.

These places are most often associated with a mountain, although there are also indications of water bodies, for example,
springs (Arriaga 1999: 119). There have been suggestions about
the existence of the concept of *pacarina* in the pre-Inca cultures
of the Sierra, but we will not discuss this issue in detail here,
since we do not have authentic written evidence (Smith 2012).

Here are some examples of mentioning *pacarinas* from
sources that allow us to specify the relevant beliefs and ideas:
"Los primeros progenitores de este ayllo Julca Tamborga que tuvieron su pacarina y nacieron del cerro grande" (Duviols 2003:
599); "los yndios que llaman llacquases tubieron su nasimiento
y pacarina de los serros nevados" (Duviols 2003: 608); "algunas

personas habían dicho, que todos los hombres no tuvieron un origen de Adan, y Eva, sino que cada Ayllo tiene diferente Pacarina, de donde proceden" (Duviols 2003: 114). It is obvious that the "big mountain" mentioned here was a particularly revered object at the local level with the status of *waka*. In principle, all cases of mentioning *pacarinas* are local in nature, that is, each of them was revered within a single community. The latter circumstance is emphasized in the third quotation, and it clearly shows the condemnation of the practice of honoring *pacarinas* from the point of view of the Christianity.

Of course, the origin of people from different *pacarinas* did not indicate a fundamentally different origin at all, just the specific embodiments of these ideas differed depending on local conditions. in this regard, it is interesting that the Lake Titicaca is sometimes represented as a *pacarina* even in communities located far from it (Duviols 2003: 400). But this is rather an exception, since the veneration of *pacarinas* required constant treatment, rituals, sacrifices, etc., in other words, direct contact with the object of veneration.

It is appropriate to mention here that mountains in the Andean worldview (and especially in the Sierra) often act as the abode of souls after death; the corresponding mentions in the ethnographic literature are extremely numerous (Sánchez-Garrafa 2015: 126; Spedding 2008: 90; Harris 1983: 146). In principle, mountains were one of the central objects of the Andean cult, which was reflected in the diversity of their veneration: on the one hand, their connection with celestial and solar cults is obvious, and on the other, the already mentioned inclusion of mountains in the Cathonic context.

In it essential to say some words regarding the connection of *pacarinas* and the afterlife. They are not directly called places of the afterlife, but in essence these concepts can be viewed as synonyms, which follows from some references in the sources:

"hasen estas honrras y cabo de año al dicho difunto para que se baya a su pacarina o vpaimarca y pueda pasar la puente de Achacaca que es de cabellos" (Duviols 2003: 364); "el alma del dicho difunto desian y tienen tradision que ba a descansar a su pacarina" (Duviols 2003: 371). Thus, both places act both as the place of origin of life (hence the close connection of the cult of ancestors with fertility, water, etc. [Sherbondy 1986: 9-12; Meconi 1999: 168; Berenguer 2000: 32]) and as the last refuge of people after death. in our opinion, the main difference between *pacarinas* and the Underworld in general is that specific *pacarinas* are special cases, a kind of separate "entrances" to the afterlife. Such an association of the place of origin of souls with their resting place is fundamentally different from the Christian concept of soul, in which these two locations do not intersect with each other. At the same time, the idea of *pacarina* as a place of origin of life and its resting place is not unique; similar ideas are observed among some other peoples.

The motif of soul rest is interesting, which is almost universally mentioned in connection with *pacarinas*. What is behind this word (descanso/descansar): an Andean concept or already a Christian influence? it is difficult to answer this question unequivocally, but we can do some considerations. Considering that in the Andean worldview, the posthumous existence was thought of as a continuation of life, it was hardly perceived as "rest" in the conventional sense of the word. However, it is possible that this term here means just a return to the origins, a reunion with the ancestors, which is what we are talking about, for example, here: "El alma del difunto y que con este sacrificio ba a descansar al nasimiento y pacarina de sus progenitores" (Duviols 2003: 415).

In connection with the above, we can raise the question of the degree of a soul's individuality in the Andean worldviews on the Underworld. The indications for this are quite contradictory. On the one hand, it is noted that people in the afterlife lead the same life as on the Earth, that is, souls continue their individual existence. On the other hand, their personal characteristics do not play any role here, since the idea of any posthumous retribution was not typical to the Andean worldview. In addition, souls are thought to be involved in the general cycle of life and death, they are closely tied to the local sacred topography at the metaphysical level. At the same time, human souls do not even have a particularly privileged status in this process, at least animal life comes from the same *pacarina* (Smith 2012: 23).

All this is fundamentally different from the status of a person and theirs soul in the Christianity where they are thought of as the crown of creation created in the image and in the likeness of God, and thus radically different from all other creatures. in turn, for the traditional Andean worldview, a human soul is a part of the macrocosm without which it cannot function normally.

Conclusions

Here we can try to answer the most important question of the paper: what is soul in the traditional Andean worldview? it is a substance that has various incarnations and acts as a reflection of a person's individuality, which continues to exist even after his death. Then comes the reunion of this substance (or part of it) with the source of its origin. The nature of the soul is contradictory, since it combines both material (the need for food, water, clothing, rest, the ability to enter into intimate relations with the living, etc.) and immaterial (the permeability, ability to take different incarnations, etc.) features.

At the present stage of development of the Andean worldview, the concept of soul has acquired a moral component (see ideas about the souls of children or sinners), but we have no doubt that it happened under the influence of the Christianity.

Despite the fragmentary nature of the available information, the following features characteristic of soul in the Andean representation can be distinguished: multiplicity; materiality; metaphoricity; close connection with the surrounding world and the sacred landscape. These features were characteristic of this concept before the beginning of the Christian influence, and they also largely remain today. in general, the Andean concept of soul can be compared with some archaic worldviews, for example, Siberian or Far Eastern ones, where the world tree was thought to be the source of all souls and where ideas about multiplicity of soul existed. All of the above was characteristic of the Andean worldview of the pre-Hispanic and partly early colonial period; subsequently, these ideas underwent a transformation towards the Christianization of indigenous peoples. However, there is no reason to talk about the complete leveling of traditional elements.

References

Alvarado Vadillo 2019 — Alvarado Vadillo D.H. Una comprensión andina del cuerpo. Lima: Multigrafik Ediciones, 2019.

Arguedas 1953 — Arguedas J.M. Cuentos mágico-realistas y canciones de fiestas tradicionales // Folklore Americano. 1953. № 1. P. 101-293.

Arguedas 2015 — Arguedas J.M. (ed.). Dioses y hombres de Huarochirí. Lima Instituto de Estudios Peruanos, 2015.

Arriaga 1999 — Arriaga P.J. de. La extirpación de la idolatría en el Perú. Cuzco: CBC, 1999.

Bascopé Caero 2001 — Bascopé Caero V. El sentido de la muerte en la cosmovisión andina: el caso de los valles andinos de Cochabamba // Chungara: Revista de Antropología Chilena. 2001. Vol. 33. № 2. P. 271-277.

Berenguer Rodriguez 2000 — Berenguer Rodriguez J. Tiwanaku: señores del lago sagrado. Santiago: Museo del arte chileno, 2000.

Calancha 1638 — Calancha A. de la. Coronica moralizada. Barcelona: Pedro Lacavalleria, 1638.

Carter 1968 — Carter W.E. Secular reinforcement in Aymara death ritual // American Anthropologist. 1968. Vol. 70. № 2. P. 238-263.

Cieza de León 2005 — Cieza de León P. de. Crónica del Perú. El señorío de los incas. Caracas: Biblioteca Ayacucho, 2005.

Cobo 1893 — Cobo B. Historia del Nuevo Mundo. T. IV. Sevilla: Imprenta de E. Rasco, 1893.

Dedenbach-Salazar Sáenz 2003 — Dedenbach-Salazar Sáenz S. Die Stimmen von Huarochirí. Indianische Quechua-Überlieferungen aus der Kolonialzeit zwischen Mündlichkeit und Schriftlichkeit. Bonn: Universität Bonn, 2003.

Duviols 2003 — Duviols P. Procesos y visitas de idolatría. Cajatambo, siglo XVII. Lima: PUCP, IEFA, 2003.

Fernández Juárez 2001 — Fernández Juárez G. Almas y difuntos: ritos mortuorios entre los aymara lacustres del Titicaca // Chungara: Revista de Antropología Chilena. 2001. Vol. 33. № 2. P. 201-219.

Fuenzalida 1977 — Fuenzalida F.V. El mundo de los gentiles y las tres eras de la creación // Revista de la Universidad Católica. 1977. № 2. P. 59-84.

Harris 1983 — Harris O. Los muertos y los diablos entre los laymi de Bolivia // Chungara: Revista de Antropología Chilena. 1983. № 11. P. 135-152.

Hocquenghem 1989 — Hocquenghem A.M. Iconografía mochica. Lima: PUCP, 1989.

Lefranc 2015 — Lefranc H.H. La vida post mórtem en la sociedad quechua del Sur Andino peruano: testimonio de una experiencia // Wiesse J. (ed.). Purgatorios, Purgatori. Lima: Fondo Editorial de la Universidad del Pacífico, 2015. P. 159-205.

Meconi 1999 — Meconi M.P. La cosmovisión religiosa andina en los documentos inéditos del Archivo Romano de la Compañía de Jesus. 1581-1752. Lima: PUCP, 1999.

Meconi 1990 — Meconi M.P. Naturaleza y funciones de los espíritus de los antepasados en el curanderismo andino del departamento de Piura // Antropologica. Vol. 8. № 8. 1990. P. 145-174.

Murúa 2011 — Murúa M. de. Historia general del Perú. Madrid: Dastin, 2001.

Ondegardo 1906 — Ondegardo P. de. Instrucción contra las ceremonias y ritos que usan los indios conforme al tiempo de su infidelidad // Revista Histórica. Lima: Opinión nacional, 1906. P. 192-203.

Onofre Mamani 2001 — Onofre Mamani L.D. Alma Imaña: rituales mortuorios en las zonas rurales aymara de Puno circumlacustre (Perú) // Chungara: Revista de Antropología Chilena. 2001. Vol. 33. Nº 2. P. 235-244.

Ortega 2001 — Ortega Pecrier M. Escatología andina: metáforas del alma // Chungara: Revista de Antropología Chilena. 2001. Vol. 33. Nº 2. P. 253-258.

Palma 1977 — Palma R. Cien tradiciones peruanas. Caracas: Biblioteca Ayacucho, 1977.

Payne 2000 — Payne J. She-calf and other Quechua folk tales. Albuquerque: University of Texas Press, 2000.

Pizarro 2013 — Pizarro P. Relación del descubrimiento y conquista de los reinos del Perú. Lima: Fondo de Cultura Económica, 2013.

Rivet, Tomasi 2016 — Rivet M.C., Tomasi J. Casitas y Casas Mochas. Los antiguos y los abuelos en sus arquitecturas (Coranzulí y Susques, provincia de Jujuy, Argentina) // L. Bugallo, M. Vilca (ed.). Wak'as, diablos y muertos: alteridades significativas en el mundo andino. San Salvador de Jujuy: Editorial de la Universidad Nacional de Jujuy — EDIUNJU; Instituto Francés de Estudios Andinos, 2014. P. 375-411.

Sánchez Garrafa 2015 — Sánchez Garrafa R. Apus de los cuatro suyus. Lima: IEP, 2015.

Santillan 1879 — Santillan F. de. Relación del origen, descendencia, política y gobierno de los incas // Tres relaciones de antigüedades peruanas. Madrid: Imprenta y fundación de M. Tello, 1879. P. 3-133.

Scherbondy 1986 — Scherbondy J.E. Mallki: ancestros y cultivo de árboles en los Andes. Lima: FAO, Ministerio de Agricultura, 1986.

Scott 2012 — Scott C.S. Generative landscapes: the step mountain motif in Tiwanaku iconography. Barnardswille: Boundary and Archaeology Research Center, 2012.

Spedding 2008 — Spedding A.P. Religión en los Andes: extirpación de idolatrías y modernidad de la fe andina. La Paz: Instituto Superior Ecuménico Andina de Teología, 2008.

Strupp Green 1980 — Strupp Green J. The day of the dead in Oaxaca, Mexico an historical inquiry // Kalish R.A (ed). Death and dying views from many cultures. Farmindale, New York: Baywood Pub Company, 1980. P. 56-71.

Ugarte 1951 — Ugarte R.V. Concilios limenses (1551-1772). Lima, 1951.

Vaderrana Fernández, Escalante Gutierrez 1980 — Vaderrana Fernández R., Escalante Gutierrez C. Apu Qorpuna: visión del mundo de los muertos en la comunidad de Awkimarka // Debates de Antropología. 1980. Nº 5. P. 233-264.

Valera 1956 — Valera B. Costumbres antiguas del Perú. México: Secretaría de Educación Pública, 1956.

van den Berg 1989 — van den Berg H. La celebración de los difuntos entre los campesinos aymaras del Altiplano // Anthropos. 1989. Bd. 3. P. 155-175.

Vilcapoma 2015 — Vilcapoma J.C. Mito y religión en Parinacochas: gentiles, Incas y cristos: documentos del siglo XVII. Lima: Argos, 2015.

van Kessel 2001 — van Kessel J. El ritual mortuorio de los aymara de Tarapacá como vivencia y crianza de la vida // Chungara: Revista de Antropología Chilena. 2001. Vol. 33. Nº 2. P. 221-234.

Beliefs Involving Parental Thoughts, Desires, and Actions and their Effects on Offspring among the Q'eqchi Maya, Hopi, and Achuar (Shiwiar)

Campbell Darby, Dr. Richard J. Chacon

Introduction

This investigation documents the presence of a particular be-lief found among three indigenous societies located respectively in North, Central, and South America. Namely, the Q'eqchi' Maya of Guatemala, the Hopi of Arizona, and the Achuar (Shiwiar) of Ecuador. The belief in question holds that parental thoughts, desires, and actions affect offspring.

The Q'eqchi' Maya of Guatemala

Darby conducted ethnographic fieldwork among the Q'eqchi' Maya that inhabit the central highlands and northern lowlands comprising the Department of Alta Verapaz along with a small section of the Peten of Guatemala. Many areas of this region are modernizing quickly and incorporating more and more aspects of Western culture into their daily lives and practices. However, in remote areas of the country, various traditional beliefs and practices remain. Examples of such practices will be drawn from two villages, Santa Lucia Lachua and Las Tortugas, both of which are located in the Department of Alta Verapaz.

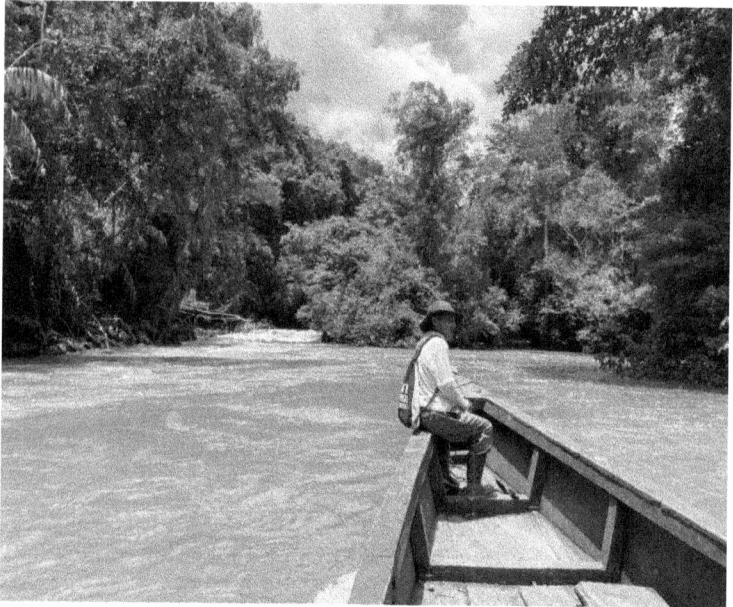

Figure 1. Campbell Darby conducting research among the Q'eqchi' Maya of Guatemala.

Awas is the traditional Q'eqchi belief which holds that the thoughts, actions, desires, likes, and dislikes of a pregnant couple can have a profound impact on their offspring. This particular belief was explained to Darby as follows "This Q'eqchi' philosophy, is part of our traditional culture that places the human being as part of the universe, our grandparents were able to decipher the behavior of the same and accommodate their life, their culture, their civilization to the rhythms of existence, what we (Q'eqchi Maya) have learned has been passed from generation to generation. The *awas*, is the feeling of the people involved (in the action, or pregnancy), should not have hatred, pity, fear, or desire for a certain thing, so as not to affect the developing baby. Meaning also that they should not have a strong emotional reaction to something that they see in a person or the environment" (Carlos Efrain Tox Tiul, personal communication to Darby, 2021).

From the early stages of pregnancy, parents will attempt to remain neutral/measured in their emotions, thoughts, likes, and dislikes with the goal being to experience no strong emotion of any sort. If the parents fail to remain circumspect, their child will be born with *awas*, which typically will manifest itself around 4 months after birth. Moreover, if the condition of *awas* is not properly diagnosed and cured, it will become permanent. It is said that the diagnosis can be difficult as the *awas* could have been transferred to the child at any point during the pregnancy and therefore, intense self-reflection on the part of the parents is called for. The cure will vary from case to case depending on the cause of the *awas*. Normally, the parents will be capable of diagnosing and curing the *awas* on their own. However, at times, more experience is called for at which point, a local shaman will be summoned.

In the following paragraphs, the specific kinds of *awas* will be examined along with the emotions and desires that caused them, as well as their cure or their failure to be cured. The first example is one known as *awas de pelotas* or the ball *awas*. a particular baby girl was born with a puffy face and large swollen cheeks in the village of Santa Lucia Lachua. Consequently, her parents came to the conclusion that this *awas* came from the father, who during the pregnancy, spent an inordinate amount of time playing soccer. Thus, it was his desire to play that transferred the round feature of the soccer ball onto his then unborn daughter's cheeks. in an effort to cure their child, the parents bought three inflatable balls, passed them over the girl's swollen cheeks and then they took these balls to a fork in the road at night and threw them over their shoulders (it is strictly forbidden for the parents to look back at the balls). After doing this, the parents returned to their home and immediately went to bed. Fortunately, this ritual had the desired effect and the baby girl has now been restored to full health with normally sized cheeks.

Another type of *awas* was recorded in the case of a woman who was living with her parents in the Las Tortugas community. When this woman was pregnant, men who worked for her father brought a turtle to the house to cook and eat. All members of the household shared in the consumption of the turtle. The baby girl appeared normal at birth but after a few months, her limbs began to grow in a deformed manner, taking on the features of a turtle. It was concluded that this *awas* caused deformity was the result of either the mother or father of the child reacting in a certain way to seeing the turtle cooked. The parents may have reacted with a strong desire to consume the turtle or they may have been thoroughly disgusted with the thought of eating the turtle. Unfortunately, according to members of the community, the parents did not take the proper steps to diagnose and to cure the *awas*, therefore, the condition became permanent.

The final examples come from a local family who reside in the aforementioned community of Santa Lucia Lachua. We will refer to the family name as Valencia.* During the course of fieldwork, Darby resided in the Valencia family home and recorded the following *awas* incident. Shortly before Darby's arrival, a baby named Joelle was born. He was a rather sickly child that was plagued with a cough and very watery/runny eyes. Joelle's grandmother, Doña Rosaria, visited her grandson and she encountered a duck (owned by Joelle's parents) that was

* in order to ensure the privacy of Q'eqchi' Maya individuals, the personal names appearing in this chapter are fictitious.

suffering from a similar eye condition (i.e. watery/runny eyes). Doña Rosaria concluded that Joelle was born with watery/runny eyes because of the presence of this particular duck. Due to this, the child's father was compelled to kill this duck, take its head, drink some of the blood and then rub its blood over Joelle's face. At midnight, the mother walked to a fork in the road and tossed the duck's head over her shoulder and immediately returned home without looking back. Just as in the aforementioned case of the girl with swollen cheeks, this ritual proved effective and Joelle's eyes ceased being watery/runny.

Reportedly, Doña Rosaria had also similarly 'cured' her own child many years before. Her son was said to have been born with "pig's feet" *awas*. This was described as a skin condition that, as the name suggests, mimics the appearance of a pig's feet. The cure was largely the same. Doña Rosaria was compelled to consume a portion of the pig's feet. She then walked to a fork in the road at midnight and tossed the feet over her shoulder for three nights in a row without ever looking back. Her son, now in his thirties (with normal feet), adamantly believes that this ritual cured him.

Despite the large amount of cultural changes that have taken place in the region, belief in *awas* remain as a prominent traditional belief among Q'eqchi' Maya.* In the next section, similar beliefs and practices recorded among the Hopi and the Achuar (Shiwiar) are presented.

* it should be noted that according to the Q'eqchi' Maya, *awas* will always be manifested in a negative way, never in a healthy manner. in other words, there is no such thing as an *awas* that has a positive effect on a child.

The Hopi of the American Southwest

The Hopi live in a relatively isolated area of northeastern Arizona and with one exception, they reside on three mesas (Woolf, Dukepo 1969). It is this isolation that has permitted the tribe to maintain many of its traditional beliefs such as their *katsina* ceremonies. One of the most enigmatic beliefs among the Hopi involves their traditional understanding of the causes of albinism.

Albinism is a condition marked by an individual's inability to produce melanin and it occurs in various populations around the world. The incidence of albinism in most human populations is about 1 in 20,000 (Hedrick 2003: 151). However, among the Hopi, 1 in 200 individuals are albino (Hedrick 2003: 151; Woolf, Dukepo 1969: 30). Such a high rate of albinism among the Hopi is odd given the deleterious effects of the condition. For example, the lack of melanin in albinos increases risk of skin cancer by 1,000-fold as is the case among the general population of Africa (Higgenson and Oettle 1960).

Health risks notwithstanding, the Hopi consider albinism to be an attractive trait and have made the following claims:

• "Albinos are considered as 'good luck charms' for a village" (cited in Woolf, Dukepo 1969: 36).

• "Albinos are smart, clean, nice, and pretty" (cited in Woolf, Dukepo 1969: 36).

• "Albino girls are very pretty" (cited in Woolf, Dukepo 1969: 36).

• "I would like to have an albino baby" (cited in Woolf, Dukepo 1969: 36).

• "I know lots of them (albinos) they are good Hopi" (cited in Woolf, Dukepo 1969: 36).

• "They (albinos) are very special" (cited in Woolf, Dukepo 1969: 36).

• "Here (on Second Mesa) we have lots of them (albinos) and we are very proud of them...We take good care of them" (cited in Woolf, Dukepo 1969: 36).

In fact, albinism is associated with purity of Hopi blood (Woolf, Dukepo 1969) and one of the effects of this traditional belief is that Hopi albinos are very popular as the following quotes indicate:

• "I knew that old (albino) man. Some say he had about twelve kids...others say about fifteen" (cited in Woolf, Dukepo 1969:36).

• "They say he (an albino) was always around trading with the ladies. He would make babies with them" (cited in Woolf, Dukepo 1969: 36).

• "He (an albino) was real funny, and knew a lot of good stories. Everyone liked him" (cited in Woolf, Dukepo 1969: 36).

Younger Hopi individuals learn that albinism is a genetic defect but traditional Hopi believe that "albinism,...is the result of some specific action in the life of the parent or close relative" (Woolf, Dukepo 1969: 36). Typical explanations for cases of albinism among the Hopi are as follows:

• "When ____ was a young man, he owned a white donkey. Everywhere he went he rode this donkey. He liked it so much two of his grandchildren were born white (albino)" (cited in Woolf, Dukepo 1969: 36).

• "____ liked to portray Eototo (white kachina). Therefore, (his daughter) was born white (albino)." (cited in Woolf, Dukepo 1969: 36).

• "____ worked with white sand while his son was being formed (and so his son was born an albino)" (cited in Woolf, Dukepo 1969: 36).

This case study reveals how traditionally, the Hopi believe that the actions of parents and/or relatives, affect unborn children. We now turn to Amazonia for more two more examples of such a belief.

the Achuar (Shiwiar) of Ecuador

Chacon studied subsistence hunting among the Achuar (Shiwiar) of the Ecuadorian Amazon and in order to gain a better understanding of native foraging practices, he often accompanied individuals on hunts (i.e. focal person follows). During the course of one foraging trip, an Achuar man named Zaca spotted a wooly monkey that was situated low in the forest canopy. Surprisingly, Zaca chose not to shoot a poisoned dart at this animal that was well within blowgun hunting range. It is important to note that up to this point of the hunt, Zaca had not bagged any game whatsoever and yet, he passed up on what could only be described as an "easy kill."

Upon returning to the village, Chacon asked Zaca, "Why didn't you shoot at that wooly monkey that was low in the forest canopy?" Zaca responded to Chacon's query by saying "You know the state that my wife is in." a puzzled Chacon asked for clarification by saying, "I know that your wife is very close to giving birth but what does this have to do with your decision to not shoot at a monkey that was in clear view?" Zaca responded by saying, "You know how we transport a dead monkey from the forest to the village... We use a jungle vine to wrap the legs and tail into a ball that is tied tightly around the neck." Zaca then added, "If I were to have killed and transported that monkey in this fashion, my wife would give birth to a child with the umbilical cord tightly wrapped around its neck and thus, my child would be dead. This is why I didn't hunt that monkey."

Figure 2. Zaca hunting with a blowgun. Photo by Chacon.

Figure 3. Zaca showing how dead monkeys are transported from the forest to the village. Photo by Chacon.

Figure 4. Close up of a dead monkey being transported from the forest to an Achuar village. Photo by Chacon.

This incident illustrates how the Achuar believe that a father's actions affect his unborn children. The effect of this belief was that Zaca passed up an opportunity to harvest a highly prized prey species because he feared that had he done so, his child would have been stillborn. It is important to point out that this Achuar belief has important theoretical repercussions for the following reason: Optimal Foraging Theory (OFT) predicts that foragers will preferentially harvest high ranked (typically large bodied) prey types over low ranked (typically small bodied) prey types (Broughton 2002; Stephens, Krebs 1986). a wooly monkey should be considered as being a relatively high ranked prey item (Chacon 2012) and yet in this instance, this Amazonian subsistence hunter (i.e. Zaca) refused to harvest this highly desired game animal. Thus, prey choice among Achuar subsistence hunters is affected in part, by non-caloric (non-energetic) factors that include the belief that a father's actions may negatively impact his unborn child. This example, notwithstanding, Chacon's (2012) findings show that OFT remains a very accurate predictor of prey choice among Achuar subsistence hunters. We now turn to another ethnographic example recorded among the Achuar.

Traditionally, the Achuar were polygynous. However, they believe that a man whose wife has just given birth, should avoid having sex with another woman for one month after delivery. Failure on the part of a father to refrain from having sex during this period may cause his newborn child to begin crying incessantly and/or to stop breastfeeding. Moreover, the infant may start vomiting, develop severe diarrhea, lose weight, and the child's ability to walk may be delayed. It is also believed that this infraction may even bring about the death of the child. The only cure for this condition is for the offending father to ingest 10 small wads of *tsaan* (tobacco) with a small amount of water. This may cause the man to become nauseous. However, in order for the treatment to be effective, the father must refrain from vomiting. Then, assuming that the father has not vomited, he will proceed to press his mouth against various parts of his child's body and sucking lightly when doing so. The father will conduct this ritual three times, once in the morning (before having breakfast), at noon, and at sundown. Each time he does this, the father is supposed to think of the woman he slept with without mentioning her name out loud. This ritual must be repeated for three days straight. After doing this, the infant will be cured. See Figure 5 for an image of an Achuar father ritually purifying his child and Figure 6 for an image of an Achuar father attempting to heal his sick child using *tsaan*. in sum, this ethnographic example further illustrates how the Achuar believe that a father's actions affect his children.

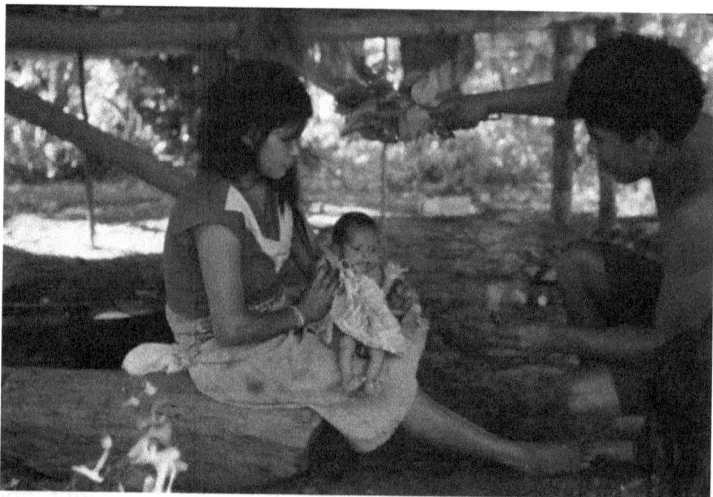

Figure 5. An Achuar man ritually purifying his child by way of a bundle of leaves referred to as a shingo-shingo. The infant is being held by its mother. Photo by Chacon.

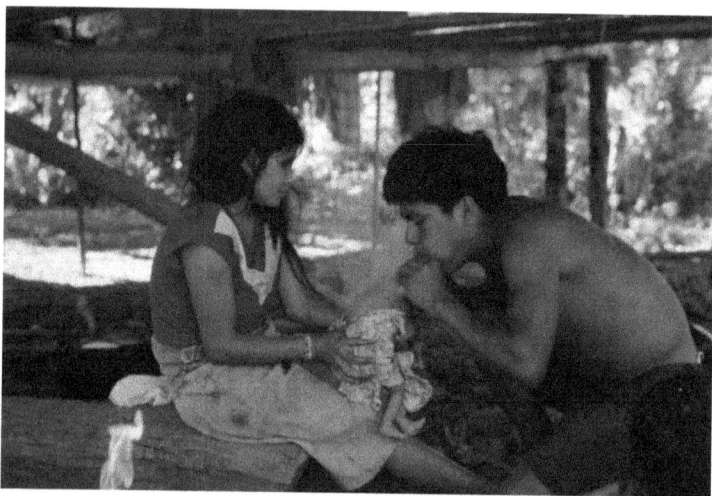

Figure 6. An Achuar man blowing tsaan (tobacco) smoke on his child in an effort to cure the infant from an illness. Photo by Chacon.

Discussion, Conclusions, and Call for Future Research

This study has shown that for the Q'eqchi Maya, Hopi, and Achuar, the beliefs, thoughts, desires, and actions of parents/relatives are believed to affect their born and unborn progeny. Since this particular belief is found among indigenous societies located in North, Central, and South America, we feel that further comparative ethnographic research is called for in order to ascertain just how widespread this particular belief is among the indigenous peoples of the Americas.

A case in point can be seen in the following example: 1 out of 200 individuals are albino among the Kuna of Panama and similar albinism rates are reported for the Jemez and Zuni of New Mexico (Woolf, Dukepo 1969: 30). The question is: Do traditional Kuna, Jemez, and Zuni believe that certain parental actions cause children to be born with albinism? With this query in mind, we call for further research into what other traits/characteristics are believed to be passed on to offspring as the result of parental thoughts, desires, and actions. Lastly, if similar versions of the belief documented in this chapter are found among other indigenous societies throughout North, Central, and South America, one of the plausible explanations for this distribution would be that this particular belief was present among Paleoindians who settled the Americas.

References

Broughton 2002 — Broughton J. Pre-Columbian Human Impact on California Vertebrates // C. Kay, R. Simmons (eds.). Wilderness and Political Ecology: Aboriginal Influences and the Original State of Nature. Salt Lake City: University of Utah Press, 2002. P. 44-71.

Chacon 2012 — Chacon R. Conservation or Resource Maximization? Analyzing Subsistence Hunting Among the Achuar (Shiwiar) of Ecuador // R. Chacon, R. Mendoza (eds.). The Ethics of Anthropology and Amerindian Research:

Reporting on Environmental Degradation and Warfare. New York: Springer, 2012. P. 311-360.

Hedrick 2003 — Hedrick P. Hopi Indians, 'cultural' selection, and albinism // American Journal of Physical Anthropology. 2003. Vol. 121(2). P. 151-6.

Higgenson, Oettle 1960 — Higgenson J., Oettle A. Cancer in the South African Bantu // Journal of the National Cancer Institute. 1960. Vol. 24. P. 643-647.

Stephens, Krebs 1986 — Stephens D., Krebs J. Foraging Theory. Princeton: Princeton University Press, 1986.

Drip, Drip, Drought: Climate Patterns at the Presidio & Mission of San Carlos de Monterey, 1770-1800

Jennifer A. Lucido

Introduction

Climatological information contributes to the understanding of climate variability and trends within a given locality or region (Mock 1991, 63). Such studies employ proxies based on oxygen isotopic analyses, ice core records, dendrochronology (tree-ring data), sediment cores, and other means to reconstruct past climate, chronicle change over time, and create predictive models (Bruckner n.d.). Documentary-based evidence (i.e., diaries, official records, personal letters, maps, etc.) of climate data can provide additional insights regarding changing environments and weather from a historical perspective (Lydon et al. 2018; Mock 1991). in turn, primary sources can inform the history of social, economic, and agricultural developments. This paleoclimatic approach is applicable to not only learning about the historical

weather conditions during the late 18th-century Spanish colonization of the Monterey Peninsula of California but also the impact of these events on the colonial landscape.

The purpose of this paper is to examine changing climate
patterns in the Monterey Peninsula during the first three decades of colonization (from approximately 1771 to 1800) of the
El Real Presidio de San Carlos de Monte Rey (hereafter the Royal
Presidio of Monterey, Presidio of Monterey, or the Presidio) and
Mission San Carlos Borromeo de Monterey (currently referred
to as Mission San Carlos de Carmelo or Carmel Mission, or Mission San Carlos), located within the Monterey Peninsula of California (see Figure 1) (Lucido 2015: 3; Lydon et al. 2018; Mock
1991: 37; Serra 1955a: 349). The time period under study falls
within the period of cool climate known as the Little Ice Age
(LIA), ca. 1400 C.E. to 1850 C.E. (Koerper et al. 1985, 1991). This
study compares multidisciplinary datasets, including the Palmer Drought Severity Index (PDSI), which informs the drought
generated from the tree-ring-based North American Drought
Atlas (NADA), Spanish colonial period weather-related observations from the documentary record, and other secondary sources to provide a cursory overview of climate conditions during
the colonization of the Monterey Peninsula and surrounding
region (Cook 2004; Lydon et al. 2018).

Spanish Colonialism in California

In the late 18th century, Spain sought to settle the land north
of New Spain or modern-day Mexico. This land would become
the Spanish colonial province known as Alta California, now
the state of California. The threat of Russian and British colonization in Alta California prompted Spanish efforts to colo-
nize the territory (Lucido 2015: 47; Lucido, Mendoza 2019: 27).
The colonization of Alta California consisted of the establishment

of religious and military settlements, referred to as a "colonial package," which was a system utilized by Spain in their global colonization efforts (Graham 1998: 29).

In the case of California, the first part of the colonial package consisted of a Franciscan missionary program. Missionization was implemented and financed in part by *Fondo Piadoso de las Californias* or Pious Fund (Lucido 2015: 47; Lucido, Mendoza 2019: 27). The objective of the Franciscan missionary effort was to evangelize the indigenous or native peoples of California. This consisted of baptizing natives and converting them to Catholicism. Such required the construction of mission settlements that would house the "new Christians" otherwise referred to as "neophytes" (Fages 1937: 64; Lucido 2015: 55). in addition, the Franciscan missionaries were tasked under the Pious Fund with the Hispanicization of the neophytes at each of the twenty-one missions of Alta California (Lucido 2015: 4; Lucido, Mendoza 2019: 27). The neophytes would thus become Spanish subjects (Lucido 2015: 117).

To protect the missions, missionaries, and neophytes, presidio or garrison settlements were also established. Four presidios were founded in Alta California, including Monterey, San Diego, Santa Barbara, and San Francisco (Lucido 2015: 5). The presidios provided military protection against potential threats from other colonial powers, such as the British or Russians. Mission guards or *escoltas* consisted of three to six soldiers assigned to each mission (Lucido 2015: 102). The primary duties of the escoltas were to protect the mission and enforce the missionization process, including retrieving neophytes who had left the mission without permission or approved leave (Lightfoot 2005: 61; Lucido 2015: 102; Schneider et al. 2012: 328).

The Spanish occupation of the Monterey region was formalized on June 3, 1770, when the joint Mission and Presidio of San Carlos settlement was founded. At the time of the Spanish arrival in Monterey Bay, two primary indigenous groups occupied the region, the Esselen and Southern Ohlone/Costanoan (Rumsen) peoples (Lucido 2015: 45; Lucido, Mendoza 2019: 37). Five primary Esselen districts or multi-village communities were identified at Spanish contact. These included *Excelen, Eslenajan, Imunajan, Ecgeajan,* and *Aspasniajan,* which spanned Carmel Valley in the northwest and other inland regions near the Arroyo Seco, Salinas River, and adjacent creeks of southeastern Monterey County (Breschini, Haversat 2004: 6; Lucido 2015: 47; Milliken 1990: 59). Esselen population size ranged from 500 to 1,300 speakers and, as such, the Esselen were among the smallest indigenous groups in California (Breschini, Haversat 2004: 5). The Rumsen territory extended from the San Francisco Bay and Carquinez Strait in the north to the Big Sur and Salinas rivers in the south (Levy 1978: 485; Lucido 2015: 47; Milliken 1995: 19). The three primary Rumsen districts identified at Spanish contact spanned the Monterey Peninsula to Big Sur River. These included *Rumsen, Ensen,* and *Sargentaruc* (Breschini and Haversat 2004: 6; Lucido 2015: 47; UCB 2013). Collectively these districts represent the Rumsen ethnolinguistic group, which consisted of approximately 800 speakers (Lucido 2015: 47; UCB 2013).

Historic Drought Analysis & NADA PDSI

The study of historic drought can document changing climate patterns and peoples' responses to such events in a given time and geographic place or region (Rowntree 1985: 7). Drought occurs when there is "below-normal precipitation often combined with warm temperatures over months to years" (Zhao, Dai 2015: 4490). However, to accurately understand historic drought, it is important to recognize that different categories may factor into climate variability. These include recognition of multiple types of drought, including not limited to 1) meteorological drought, defined as "the departure from statistical norms" (Rowntree 1985: 7–8); 2) drought as the result of "socially induced water shortages," such as agricultural production which impacts soil moisture levels (Rowntree 1985: 7–8; Xianfeng et al. 2016: 752); 3) low river flow conditions and/or decrease in aquifer levels, which may cause hydrological drought (Xianfeng et al. 2016: 752); and 4) socio-economic drought, which may arise from imbalances from either agricultural or hydrological conditions (Xianfeng et al. 2016: 752).

Temperature and precipitation data from PDSI and NADA are important to estimate drought and relative dryness (Cook 2004; Palmer 1965: 45; Zhao, Dai 2015: 4491). The index spans conditions of extreme wetness to extreme dryness or drought, applying a scale of + 4.0 or greater to -4.0 or less. Environmental scientists, climatologists, geographers, and other scholars have traditionally used PDSI to record meteorological drought; furthermore, atmospheric scientists Tianbao Zhao and Aiguo Dai (2015, 4491) argue that the PDSI should also be utilized to measure agricultural drought. However, there are limitations to the application of PDSI because it operates within a fixed time scale (i.e., monthly) and cannot account for the calibration of local climate (Guttman 1998: 113; Xianfeng et al. 2016: 753–754). Therefore, dendroclimatic data represent relative levels of rainfall rather than the distribution of rain in a given year (Jackson, Gardzina n.d.).

While this paper relies on various datasets of PDSI and NADA (sometimes referred to as NADA PDSI), it should be noted that new indexes have since emerged as more precise measurements of wet conditions, including the Standardized Precipitation Index (SPI), the crop moisture index (CMI), and a host of other meteorological and agricultural drought monitoring indices (Guttman 1998: 113; Xianfeng et al. 2016: 753-754). Historian Sam White (2019, 1810) also observes that when using NADA

PDSI, it is important to recognize that there are limitations when comparing it with the documentary record. First is the fact that NADA is an imperfect reconstruction of drought conditions. Second, there are likely discrepancies between NADA PDSI reconstructions with first-hand accounts. However, White cautions that such disagreements do not necessarily negate one form of data over another. Even so, frequent variation may suggest issues of reliability of a given primary source or the lack of precision of the NADA reconstruction (White 2019, 1810). in contrast, White contends that "consistent agreement (between the historical record and NADA) should build confidence in both" and therefore provides further understanding of climate change (2019, 1810).

Overview of Dry Years in Alta California

Distinguishing between different types of droughts in the context of Alta California during the Mission era is particularly challenging. This is because the size of California encompasses different climate divisions (CD) that span different gradients of precipitation (He et al. 2017: 1778–1779). Geophysical researchers He et al. (2017: 1778–1779) identify seven classifications of CD in California: CD1: North Coast drainage; CD2: Sacramento drainage; CD3: Northeast Interior drainage; CD4: Central Coast drainage; CD5: San Joaquin drainage; CD6: South Coast drainage; and CD7: Southeast Desert drainage. The Presidio and Mission of San Carlos fall within the CD4: Central Coast drainage, which is associated with a Mediterranean climate with dry summers and wet winters (He et al. 2017: 1778). As such, normal precipitation can vary significantly concerning time and space combined with the environmental impacts associated with the adaptive strategies of colonial populations, particularly that of their agricultural and economic activities (Allen 2010: 70;

Rowntree 1985: 8). Given this, recognizing the various types of rainfall in California is also important.

In his drought analysis study during the mission period in California, environmental geographer Lester Rowntree (1985: 8) identifies six attributes of rainfall. These include 1) strong probability of drought in the summer due to imbalances between evaporation, transpiration, and precipitation; 2) short occurrences of dry spells during winter rainfall which can adversely impact crop maturation or cultivation; 3) years in which there is winter rainfall with low precipitation (aka seasonal drought); 4) instances of dry periods following multiple rainfall seasons or below-average rainfall; 5) overall high variability from year-to-year. However, areas in southern California that were occupied by the Spanish demonstrate further variability, notably that of Los Angeles, Santa Barbara, San Diego, and San Luis Obispo; missions founded in these coastal areas have the lowest level of rainfall regularity and predictability; and 6) recognition of the high amount of spatial variability (Rowntree 1985: 8). The challenge for scholars thus remains as to how to distinguish and interpret such rainfall events in the Spanish colonial documentary record (Lydon et al. 2018; Rowntree 1985: 9).

In addition to contextualizing the types of rainfall, Rowntree reviewed dry years in Alta California, based on the existing PDSI and tree-ring data published in the 1970s and 1980s (1985: 14). The mission period dates presented in Figure 2 represent the ending of the tree-growing season which also corresponds with the end of the rainfall season in California (Rowntree 1985: 14). For example, drought typically indicates PDSI values of -2.0 or lower, whereas moderate to severe wet conditions are PDSI values of 2.0 or higher (Meko et al. 1980; Rowntree 1985: 14). However, Rowntree notes that PDSI values can represent wetness from a previous rainfall season and reflect conditions from the autumn of the year prior through the spring of the following year (1985: 15). This is evident for the year 1777 and its PDSI value of −5.5, and perhaps also for the year 1782 and given its PDSI value of −6.0 (Meko et al. 1980; Rowntree 1985: 14). This contrasts from 1790 to 1795 when the dry conditions appear to have increased over time (Meko et al. 1980; Rowntree 1985: 14).

When comparing tree-ring indices of big cone spruce or big cone Douglas-fir (*Pseudotsuga macrocarpa*) independent of the PDSI, Rowntree found other trends (1985, 14–15). Tree-ring indices significantly higher or lower than 1.0 constituted a clear departure from average tree-ring growth conditions (see Figure 3; Douglas 1976: 163; Rowntree 1985: 14). For example, the tree-ring index value for 1777 is 0.39, thereby suggesting subnormal rainfall during the winter of 1776–1777 (Douglas 1976: 163; Rowntree 1985: 14). This pattern appears again in 1782 (tree-ring index value 0.28), 1795 (tree-ring index value 0.29), and subsequent years during the 1800s. Presumably, the growth-limiting factor resulted from the lack of moisture associated with drought or dry conditions. a comparison of the PDSI values with the tree-ring indices (see Figure 4) demonstrates dry year patterns, particularly in the years 1777–1778, 1782–1783, and 1795-1796 (Rowntree 1985: 15-16). This suggests that the droughts from the earlier year may have impacted the next. However, Rowntree also notes that "local site and ecological factors, such as the vulnerability of moisture-stressed trees to other growth-limiting factors (e.g., parasitic infestation), could also account for this phenomenon" (1985: 15–16).

In a climate study of California precipitation by Eugene R. Wahl et al. (2020), they examined year-to-year extreme "flips" from 1571 to circa 2020. Flips consist of transitions from dry-to-wet (DW) or wet-to-dry (WD). Furthermore, Wahl et al. (2020: 10232) examined the relationship between these DW and WD flips with that of anthropogenic effects on weather and climate in California. Wahl et al. (2020) found that the flips did not appear to be associated with "enhanced anthropogenic forcing" examined during the circa 450-year period under study. Rather, Wahl et al. (2020, 10235) argued that the flip behavior in California appears to be a "quasi-random" characteristic of precipitation occurring in periods of either low or high variability. For example, there were notable periods of variability in northern and central California during the 1570s to 1580s, the late 1700s to early 1800s, and the 1820s to 1830s (Wahl et al. 2020: 10227; Wise and Dannenberg 2014).

Similar studies have also found that the period before the 1800s was characterized by "fluctuating climate conditions rather than a sustained, uniform climate period" (Wise and Dannenberg 2014: 4). This suggests that earlier anthropogenic forcing, that of the Spanish colonization of the Monterey Peninsula and California more broadly, did not have a significant or long-term impact on climate change and variability. Therefore, changing climate patterns documented in Spanish colonial records and primary sources provide insight into how naturally occurring DW and WD conditions impacted the indigenous and colonial populations of the Monterey Peninsula and their responses to it.

Reconstructed PDSI JJA & the Documentary Record

To examine climate change and patterns, the World Meteo-rological Organization (WMO) uses consecutive periods of 30 years to establish climatological standard normals (2011: 4–16). the climatological standard normals are averages based on climatological data, which serve as reference periods that allow for comparison across different regions through time (WMO 2011: 4–16). These reference periods begin on the first day of January in the first year of any given decade and end on the last day of December in the thirtieth year (WMO 2011: 4–16). For example, consecutive reference periods of the Mission and Presidio of San Carlos and the broader Monterey Bay Area begin 1 January 1771 to 31 December 1800, 1 January 1801 to 31 December 1830, and so forth. Therefore, while the year 1770 is included in this study because it is the founding year of the joint Mission and Presidio of San Carlos de Monterey, the associated climatological data with that year is not part of the 30-year reference period related to climatological standard normals (Lucido 2015: 2, 70–71; Serra 1955a: 171). Furthermore, the PDSI value of "severe drought" in 1770 is an example of either meteorological or hydrological drought as the Mission and Presidio of San Carlos had not yet sufficient time to establish agricultural conditions that would result in socio-economic drought (see Figure 5).

A review of the reference period under study suggests that from 1771 to 1800, the Mission and Presidio of San Carlos, as well as the broader Monterey Bay area, exhibited an influx of climate change (Dai, National Center for Atmospheric Research 2019; NADA 2018). As shown in Figure 5, within the 30-year period, 14 years reflect "nearly normal conditions" as per their assigned PDSI value of zero, whereas the remaining 16 demonstrate deviation from those conditions.* of the 16 years demonstrating deviation from nearly normal conditions, eight represent dry years (moderate to extreme drought), whereas the remaining eight are wet years (moderate to extreme wetness). The dry or drought years include the 1776–1777, 1782–1783, 1788, 1794–1795, and 1800 and the wet years include 1784–1785, 1787, 1789–1790, 1792, 1797, and 1799.

---

* the PDSI values presented in Figure 5 are approximate and do not reflect exact values. For example, nearly normal conditions fall within the PDSI value range of -1.9 to 1.9 but have been replaced with values of "0" for illustrative purposes.

Arrival to the Monterey Bay, 1770

After arriving by land to the Monterey Peninsula on May 23, 1770, eight days before the arrival of Father Junípero Serra to the Monterey Bay, who was aboard the *San Antonio,* Juan Crespí documented some of the earliest weather observations about the Mission and Presidio of San Carlos (Crespí and Brown 2001: 731, 737; Serra 1955a: 161). Crespí noted that (written circa November 11, 1770):

> From the day after reaching this spot (an inlet by the Monterey Bay), the 6th (of June), we had about two days' worth of fine rain. We have not had any more rain since we became settled down here at the Harbor of Monte Rey...we have noticed a great deal of chill during the month of May when we arrived, and June, July, August, and September. The winds commence to die down about the middle of September, after being very strong and chill and continuous throughout the aforesaid months, with most of the days being very overcast with a very dense fog, without sight of the sun, and with a very strong northwest wind that almost always continues both day and night. And through the west and southwest winds commonly blow just as chill as this...(Crespí and Brown 2001: 741)

This description of the lack of rain appears to be consistent with the PDSI severe drought of 1770 from June through August (see Figure 6). The next rainfall was not until October 15, 1770 (Crespí and Brown 2001: 741). Crespí described the fall rainfall as "harder" because it penetrated the soil and prompted seed growth. Rain appeared again in November, accompanied by a strong wind and chill that evidently "withered some things in Don Pedro (Fages) the Lieutenant's garden," including beans, tomatoes, and other garden greens (Crespí and Brown 2001: 741).

However, as previously noted, 1770 is not part of the 30-year period. Nevertheless, the corroboration between the documentary record and the NADA PDSI value for 1770 is worth noting.

1771–1775

From 1771 to 1775, the general climate in the Monterey Peninsula and the general bay area were relatively consistent as per the NADA PDSI values (see Figure 7) (NADA 2018; Dai, National Center for Atmospheric Research 2019). The reconstructed JJA PDSI reflects nearly normal conditions during these five years, although there was a slight movement towards a wetter climate, except in the year of 1772. in Pedro Fages' description of California, he reported within the timeframe noted that at Mission San Carlos:

> The planting of corn turned out well, and the same is hoped of the wheat, although all that is sown will always be exposed to the usual risks of excess or lack of rain, or of being sown out of season, since there is no means of taking irrigating water out of the river because the water flows deep in it and confine within a narrow bed. (Fages 1937: 81)

This essentially correlates to reconstructed JJA PDSI. The apparent lack of evident deviation from the normal weather--wet or dry conditions — as observed by Fages, suggests a stable climate within the five-year period.

Despite Fages' positive report, the initial agricultural endeavors near Mission San Carlos, which had been relocated near the Carmel River in 1771, did not yield successful harvests (Beebe and Senkewicz 2015: 221; Smith et al. 2017: 161; Serra 1955a: 241). These inadequate crops were not the result of the dry or wet climate but rather a severe miscalculation of fertile soil. On June 21, 1771, Serra explained in a letter to Father Francisco Palou the error of judgment concerning the absence of viable agricultural land:

What we did here—we of the mission—in the way of raising crops came to nothing. We made a little garden nearby, and enclosed it; the Indians did the digging. The whole of it became one seeding bed, as Father Fray Juan had all kinds of seeds. Everything came out fin , but nothing grew to maturity. We were all greatly puzzled. Later we found out that the ground, while showing no signs of it, at times is washed over by the salt water of the bay, and so is fit for nothing but nettles and reeds.

As regards (to) the presidio—Don Pedro had two gardens; one produced plenty of cabbages and other vegetables; the other still more, even a little wheat and barley. But now that we are going to Carmel we hope things well (sic) be different. (Serra 1955a: 241)

Over a year later, on August 8, 1772, Serra reported that "With regard to crops nothing worthy of the name has as yet been achieved" (Serra 1955a: 257). in the same report, Serra noted that his fellow Franciscan missionary, Juan Crespí, described the Monterey Bay area as uninhabitable "on account of the extreme cold, fogs, and bad weather" and requested immediate removal (Serra 1955a: 251). Serra continued to describe Crespí's "dissatisfaction with the climate" in which Crespí claimed that "bad though it was in Monterey, in Carmel it was still worse; that it was still colder here (in Carmel)" (Serra 1955a: 251). Despite the apparent bad weather, 1772 marked one of the earliest documentation of a successful crop at Mission San Carlos, of which a mere eight bushels of wheat were harvested (Engelhardt 1934: 244; Smith et al. 2017: 161–162).

While drought did not appear to contribute to the success or lack thereof of agricultural production at the Presidio and Mission San Carlos as per the reconstructed JJA PDSI, it was an issue during these early years of colonization. This was exacerbated by the fact that no supply ships were sent to Alta California, in 1773 (Engelhardt 1934: 41; Geiger 1955: 144; Kemp 2010: 59; Smith et al. 2017: 162). To that end, Palou described the conditions from 1773 to early 1774 at Mission San Carlos and Monterey more generally:

> The worst kind of a famine that was ever endured in the regions about Monterey visited us. For eight months milk was the manna for all from the comandante and the Fathers down to the least individual; and I shared it with the rest...At this Mission of San Carlos for thirty-seven days we were without a tortilla or as much as a crumb of bread. The meals consisted of a gruel made of garvanzos (sic) or beans ground to flour with which milk was mixed. in the morning a little coffee took the place of chocolate. (Engelhardt 1934: 41–42)

As a result, to supplement dietary subsistence at Mission San Carlos, the Rumsen and Esselen neophytes were given *paseos* or approved leave for hunting, fishing, and gathering of seeds (Engelhardt 1934: 42; Lightfoot 2005: 61; Smith et al. 2017: 162).

During this period, the presence of rain proved problematic for maintaining mission buildings at Carmel (Williams 1993: 16). Initially, thatch was used for roofing the mission buildings at Carmel and the Presidio. This was then replaced with flat earth coverings, or *azoteas*, a common type of roof structure used in other parts of New Spain (Williams 1993: 16). However, the wetter season of 1771 proved to create problems with this type of roofing for the buildings at Carmel.

To that end, the Spanish Franciscan missionary Francisco Palóu observed that:

...They have just finished building another church about thirty varas long (at Carmel), partly of logs and partly of planks, with a roof of tule because it has been experienced that the flat roof does not bear heavy rains, to serve until such time as a skilled master can be obtained to build it as the country requires... (Palóu 1926, 231)

Even though the azoteas were equipped with waterspouts, the wet climate at the time rendered them "totally impractical" (Williams 1993: 38). As a result, grass and reed construction roofs became popular not only in Monterey but throughout Alta California, for temporary roofing of new buildings (Williams 1993: 39). However, these types of roofs were also dangerous as they were more susceptible to fires. Roof tiles eventually came to replace the thatch roofing in the presidio buildings.

1776 & 1777

The following two years proved to be drastically different concerning NADA PDSI records. The reconstructed JJA PDSI indicates that conditions became increasingly dry, measuring from moderate drought in 1776 to severe drought in 1777 (see Figures 8 and 9) (NADA 2018; Dai, National Center for Atmospheric Research 2019). These droughts, in turn, impacted the agricultural output of Mission San Carlos. On April 13, 1776, Serra expressed his concern to Father Francisco Pangua about the potential loss of agricultural production at the mission:

If the boat be delayed, and an attack is made on the provisions of the missions, it will be pitiful, especially here, where we are

Lucido / Drip, Drip, Drought: Climate Patterns at the Presidio & Mission of San Carlos de Monterey, 1770–1800 facing the prospect of a bad harvest, since this year we have had less rain than at any time since we came here. Because of it the wheat, which had never before appeared so promising, is now drying up. We are having public prayers for rain; if it does not rain, we are, as far as we can see, in a terrible plight. (Serra 1955b: 419)

The following year on February 26, 1777, Serra reported a similar concern to Pangua:

Mission San Carlos harvested but little, on account of the great drought; but we have enough to give out atole twice a day to the people, and pozole once a day. And this we go on doing. (Serra 1955c: 97)

The drought of 1777 was likely the cumulative result of the lack of rainfall from the previous season in 1776. This appears to be consistent with regional drought throughout California, during which time the colonial landscape was undergoing a spectrum of dry conditions (Cook, Krusic 2004). in another account later that year, on June 1, 1777, Serra reiterated the severe drought conditions at Mission San Carlos to the Viceroy of New Spain, Antonio María de Bucareli y Ursúa:

This year has been extremely dry. That is why, in San Diego, the harvest will amount to nothing, in San Antonio, to very little, and in San Carlos, while we have worked harder than ever to sow a large acreage, my judgment is that we will not have a third of the wheat that would ordinarily be expected. And so, in order not to be dependent, as we have been until now, on the rains, and the excellence of the Land, which is indeed great, we have, for more than a month and a half now, been busy with the help of more than thirty workmen leading off the water of the

Carmel River, more than a league away. As a result, we will be able to irrigate as much ground as the mission will be capable of putting under seed for many years to come.

If we succeed in this enterprise, as I hope we will, not only will our troubles cease, but we will even be able to help many others in their difficulties. (Serra 1955c: 145 & 147)

The irrigation from the Carmel River is important to note. While the creation of the irrigation system to Mission San Carlos was a necessary reaction to the drought of 1777, which was most likely the result of meteorological and/or agricultural drought, the human or anthropogenic water management described by Serra may have impacted river flow conditions during a later period in time (Xianfeng et al. 2016: 752). As a result, this short-term solution may have had the potential to result in a more long-term issue with hydrological drought for the mission. Furthermore, interference by way of irrigation from water sources, such as rivers, can disrupt the existing ecosystems and biodiversity of a given region or area. However, none was found during this study (Lindberg et al. 2002: 925).

1778–1781

The years 1778 to 1781 remained relatively consistent as per the reconstructed JJA PDSI (see Figure 10) (NADA 2018; Dai, National Center for Atmospheric Research 2019). Conditions in the Monterey Peninsula and bay area were nearly normal during this period despite earlier periods of drought. Despite this, there were still occasional dilemmas associated with the weather.

On August 19, 1778, Serra wrote from Mission San Carlos to Father Rafael Verger to report on the status of the missions and document other concerns. in his letter, Serra described the different types of crops harvested from the missions, of which Mission San Carlos struggled in large part due to weather-related conditions:

> In the mission here (Mission San Carlos), we put in fi e fanegas of barley in seed; from that, and from some that came up without sowing, we put in the granary 508 fanegas, measured not with scrupulous exactness but running over. Of wheat, from 18 fanegas of seed, we have more than we have ever seen before. But while it was growing to maturity, there were a few cold foggy days, to which we paid no attention because externally, it did not affect the grain. When the time for reaping came however, empty ears were found, and others were not full grown. The result is that our harvest can be put down at half what it would have been and what we expected. But we are well pleased with what God gives, and I hope we will not go hungry.
>
> Besides what I have described, we harvested: lentils, six fanegas and some almuds; peas, thirteen fanegas and some almuds; horse beans, ten fanegas less two almuds. Still to be harvested: the corn and the beans; they promise well, but there have been a number of setbacks, and thieving is breaking out. The harvests have been realized, notwithstanding the setback of weather I have described, and without irrigation. We are in hopes of continuing with our project to dam the river, in order that all our land may be irrigated should the need arise. (Serra 1955c: 245-247)

Also, during this period, the cattle population had stabilized. However, their impact on the landscape resulted in the overgrazing of native grasses and seeds such that wild game populations were reduced in Monterey (Smith et al. 2017: 162). Consequently, some herds were relocated from Monterey to the Pueblo de Los Angeles.

In 1781, the indigenous people of Mission San Carlos were tasked with constructing an irrigation system, presumably the same irrigation project noted in Serra's August 1778 letter (Hackel 2005: 73). The irrigation project was completed in December 1781 after seven months of labor. During that process, native peoples also worked to create new fields for crops. in his July 1, 1784, report, Serra described the difficulties with the irrigation construction, considering that the land was "covered with long tough grasses and thickets but also with great trees, willows, alders, and so forth" (Hackel 2005: 73; Serra 1955d: 269, 273).

1782–1796

During the years between 1782 to 1796, the pattern of consecutive years of nearly normal conditions ceased at the Presidio and Mission of San Carlos (see Figures 11, 12, and 13) (NADA 2018; Dai, National Center for Atmospheric Research 2019). Rather weather conditions oscillated between nearly normal, wet, and dry. Of these three primary conditions, nearly normal conditions were the least frequently occurring. in their 1784 report on the missions, Serra and Father Mathías Antonio de Santa Cathalina Noriega wrote that in the year 1782 at Mission San Carlos:

> Towards the end of the past year 31 fanegas of barley were sown and 53 of wheat. The barley was planted where the water could not reach it and as the drought was great, it was lost. This has never happened before in the case of this grain. We gathered only 107 fanegas.

> The wheat which was irrigated did well but less than what was harvested the preceding year for the same reason and there were large stretches of sown land where (the major-domo) did not attempt to gather a single head. (Serra 1955d: 269)

The reconstructed JJA PDSI for the year 1782 undoubtedly reflects this devastation by drought at the Presidio and Mission of San Carlos (NADA 2018; Dai, National Center for Atmospheric Research 2019). The 1782 tree-ring reconstructed drought for North America indicates a regional drought that extends beyond the surrounding Monterey Bay area, as much of California in that year was under extremely dry conditions (see Figure 14) (Cook, Krusic 2004). Considering this, the drought was likely the result of naturally occurring events associated with rainfall deficit rather than caused by the introduction of Spanish colonial water and land management.

Despite the lack of grain production, Robert Jackson and Anne Gardzina (n.d.) determined that such did not have a negative impact on the indigenous population at Mission San Carlos during this period. Jackson and Gardzina (n.d.) conducted two statistical tests, regression and correlation, of twenty-year samples of data on the population and total grain production at five different missions, including Missions San Diego (est. 1769), San Gabriel (est. 1771), San Antonio (est. 1771), San Carlos, and Santa Clara (est. 1777). The years selected included 1785–1804 and 1812–1831. While the later sample is outside of the reference period for this study, it is worth noting that Jackson and Gardzina (n.d.) found that there was a statistically insignificant relationship between population size and agricultural output for these mission sites. Instead these missions collectively reflected a decrease in grain production and an increase in population size (Jackson, Gardzina n.d.).

In addition to climate-related impacts on agricultural production, weather conditions in the Monterey region also influenced architectural development and maintenance (Williams 1993: 91). According to Spanish colonial specialist, Jack S. Williams, "Prior to 1792, the ships that supplied Monterey deposited their cargos at the beach. The supplies were then transferred to the main base by cart or mule. As a result of unpredictable weather, the goods were sometimes water damaged" (1993: 91). To remedy this loss of goods, a storehouse was constructed at the landing site between 1792 and 1798 to house the supply ship cargo.

The years following 1782 inconsistently alternated between dry and wet conditions based on the reconstructed JJA PDSI (see Figures 11, 12, and 13). As previously discussed, 1795 proved to be a record drought for Monterey and California more broadly (Diaz, Wahl 2015: 4645; Wahl et al. 2020: 10227). According to historian Steven Hackel, the missionaries and soldiers were "fully aware by the mid-1790s that the Monterey region's natural environment was in a period of transformation and crisis" (2005: 78). Despite earlier efforts to relocate herds to the Pueblo de Los Angeles, the number of cattle and sheep at Mission San Carlos had significantly increased in the early 1790s. Furthermore, their numbers were growing in neighboring parts of the region.

Moreover, it was observed by soldiers of the Presidio of San Carlos that the region "had not seen rain in years" (Hackel 2005: 78). Consequently, the area became overgrazed, and native vegetation was severely reduced and damaged. Drought occurred in the region in 1793, 1794, and 1795, resulting in "inadequate pasture" to support the number of herds (Hackel 2005: 78).

1797–1800

Rains returned to Monterey and California more generally in 1798 (see Figure 15) (Hackel 2005: 79). These new rains supported the growth of non-native grasses and thousands of horses, cattle, and sheep. The "wet but cool winters" allowed the Monterey region to become a "pastoral paradise" (Hackel 2005: 79). The non-native plants introduced by Spanish colonists were able to adapt to drought conditions and support the "aggressive graz-ing" of their livestock (Hackel 2005: 79). By 1800, the Missions of San Carlos, Santa Cruz, Soledad, and San Bautista collective-ly supported some 3,811 cattle, 11,082 sheep, and 2,678 hors-es. However, this caused the displacement of native plants and forced those communities of indigenous people of Monterey who had not yet been subjected to missionization to relocate to the Spanish missions in the area.

These same rains also impacted the buildings associated with the Presidio of Monterey (Williams 1993: 91). The store-house constructed on the beach between 1792 to 1798 suffered weather-related damage in 1798. According to Williams, these storms "ripped through the (Monterey) settlement" (1993: 91). Repairs of the storehouse were not completed until the end of December of 1801.

Conclusion

Examining late 18th-century Spanish colonial period accounts provides insight into changing climate patterns of the Monterey Peninsula. Such documentation illuminates historical weather conditions and how such impacted colonization efforts. The data presented in this paper show that the wet-to-dry and dry-to-wet flips directly affected Spanish colonial efforts in the Monterey area. The ability to cultivate viable agricultural land and sustain pasture for livestock was an ongoing struggle at the Mission and Presidio of San Carlos. The introduction of agriculture and cattle by Spanish colonists undoubtedly exacerbated drought condi-tions. However, the adverse effects of drought were not the result of colonial anthropogenic forcing during the 30-year reference climatological period of this study. Rather, the oscillation be-tween drought and precipitation conditions naturally occurred in Monterey and the state of California more broadly.

Undoubtedly, a great deal more data in the historical record is yet to be addressed in a research endeavor such as this. Future studies should further document and examine changing climate patterns surrounding the Monterey Bay area during the first three decades of colonization. To that end, future research should more thoroughly investigate additional primary sources of other Spanish colonial contemporaries associated with the Mission and Presidio of San Carlos for each year within the 30-year reference period. in that way, researchers can either build higher levels of consistency or identify discrepancies concerning weather-related observations in the documentary record and NADA PDSI data. Furthermore, future studies should compare the Mission San Carlos harvest reports and associated agricultural data with the PDSI and tree-ring records. in addition, incorporating indigenous perspectives on drought and precipitation would further inform changing climate patterns. The potential findings may have important implications for drought mitigation and management in California's past, present, and future (He et al. 2017: 1784).

References

Allen 2010 — Allen R. Alta California Missions and the Pre-1849 Transformation of Coastal Lands // Historical Archaeology. 2010. Vol. 44, no. 3. P. 69-80.

Beebe, Senkewicz 2015 — Beebe R.M., Senkewicz R.M. Junípero Serra: California, Indians, and the Transformation of a Missionary. Before Gold; v. 3. Norman, Oklahoma: University of Oklahoma Press, 2015.

Breschini, Haversat 2004 — Breschini G., Haversat T. The Esselen Indians of the Big Sur Country: the Land and the People. Salinas, California: Coyote Press, 2004.

Bruckner n.d. — Bruckner M. Paleoclimatology: How Can We Infer Past Climates? // Microbial Life — Educational Resources. URL: https://serc.carleton.edu/microbelife/topics/proxies/paleoclimate.html (15.11.2019).

Burnette 2018 — Burnette D.J. The Paleoclimatology: Climate Proxies Tree-Ring

Drought Atlas Portal: a suite of research and education webtools for gridded drought reconstructions over the past 500-2000 years. American Meteorological Society Annual Meeting, Austin, TX, 2018.

Cook, Krusic 2004 — Cook E.R., Krusic P.J. The North American Drought Atlas // Lamont-Doherty Earth Observatory and the National Science Foundation. URL: https://iridl.ldeo.columbia.edu/SOURCES/.LDEO/.TRL/.NADA2004/.pdsi-atlas.html.

Crespí, Brown 2001 — Crespí J., Brown A.K. a Description of Distant Roads: Original Journals of the First Expedition into California, 1769-1770. San Diego, CA: San Diego State University Press, 2001.

Dai, National Center for Atmospheric Research 2019 — Dai, Aiguo & National Center for Atmospheric Research Staff (Eds). The Climate Data Guide: Palmer Drought Severity Index (PDSI). Last modified 23 Oct 2019. URL: https://climatedataguide.ucar.edu/climate-data/palmer-drought-severity-index-pdsi.

UCB 2013 — Department of Linguistics, University of California Berkeley (UCB). The Survey of California and Other Indian Languages. 2013. URL: http://linguistics.berkeley.edu/~survey/languages/california-languages.php (28.10.2013).

Diaz, Wahl 2015 — Diaz H.F., Wahl E.R. Recent California water year precipitation deficits: a 440-year perspective // Journal of Climate. 2015. Vol. 28. P. 4637–4652.

Douglas 1976 — Douglas A. Past Air-Sea Interaction over the Eastern North Pacific Ocean as Revealed by Tree Ring Data. Ph.D. dissertation. University of Arizona, 1976.

Engelhardt 1934 — Engelhardt Z. Mission San Carlos Borromeo (Carmelo): the Father of the Missions. Missions and Missionaries of California. New series. Local history. Santa Barbara: the Schauer Printing Studio, 1934.

Fages 1937 — Fages P. a Historical, Political and Natural Description of California by Pedro Fages. Berkeley: University of California Press, 1937.

Geiger 1955 — Geiger M. Palou's Life of Fray Junipero Serra. Washington: Academy of American Franciscan History, 1955.

Graham 1998 — Graham E. Mission Archaeology // Annual Review of Anthropology.

1998. Vol. 2. P. 25-62.

Guttman 1998 — Guttman N.B. Comparing the Palmer Drought Index and the Standardized Precipitation Index // Journal of the American Water Resources Association. 1998. Vol. 34 no. 1. P. 113-121.

Hackel 2005 — Hackel S.W. Children of coyote, missionaries of Saint Francis: Indian-Spanish relations in colonial California, 1769-1850. University of North Carolina Press, 2005.

He et al. 2017 — He X., Wada Y., Wanders N., Sheffield J. Intensification of hydrological drought in California by human water management // Geophys. Res. Lett. 2017. No. 44. P. 1777–1785.

Jackson, Gardzina n.d. — Jackson R., Gardzina A. Agriculture, Drought, and Chumash Congregation in California Missions (1782-1834). California Missions Foundation, 2017. URL: http://californiamissionsfoundation.org/articles/agriculturedroughtandchumashcongregation/.

Kemp 2010 — Kemp A. Stormy Seas in the Era of Gálvez, 1766-1774: the Naval Department of San Blas, Seasonal Weather Patterns and the Fate of the 'Monterey Expedition' // Boletin: the Journal of the California Mission Studies Association. 2010. Vol. 27 no. 1-2. P. 28-68.

Koerper et al. 1985 — Koerper H.C., Killingley J.S., Taylor R.E. The Little Ice Age and Coastal Southern California Human Economy // Journal of California and Great Basin Anthropology. 1985. Vol. 7 no. 1. P. 99-103.

Levy 1978 — Levy R.L. Costanoan // Handbook of North American Indians. Vol. 8. California. Washington, DC: Smithsonian Institution, 1978. P. 485-495.

Lightfoot 2005 — Lightfoot K.G. Indians, Missionaries, and Merchants: the Legacy of Colonial Encounters on the California Frontiers. Berkeley: University of California Press, 2005.

Lindberg et al. 2002 — Lindberg N., Engtsson J., Persson T. Effects of experimental irrigation and drought on the composition and diversity of soil fauna in a coniferous stand // Journal of Applied Ecology. 2002. Vol. 39. P. 925-936.

Lucido 2015 — Lucido J.A. The Old Stand: a Historic Resource Study of the Royal Presidio of Monterey, 1770 — 1840. Master's thesis. Sonoma State University, 2015.

Lucido, Mendoza 2019 — Lucido J.A., Mendoza R.G. The Best Port One Could

Desire: the Land and Sea Borne Quest to Establish the Real Presidio de San Carlos de Monterey, 1602-1770 // Boletin: the Journal of the California Missions Foundation. 2019. Vol. 35 no. 1. P. 12-43.

Lydon et al. 2018 — Lydon S.E., Mendoza R.G., Lucido J.A. Ramifications of the Little Ice Age on the Spanish Missions of California. Paper presented at the Society for California Archaeology Conference, San Diego, CA, March 2018.

Meko et al. 1980 — Meko D., Stockton C., Boggess W. a Tree-Ring Reconstruction of Drought in Southern California // Water Resources Bulletin. 1980. Vol. 16. P. 594-600.

Milliken 1990 — Milliken R. Ethnogeography and Ethnohistory of the Big Sur District, California State Park System, During the 1770-1810 Time Period. Submitted to Department of Parks and Recreation, Sacramento. 1990.

Milliken 1995 — A Time of Little Choice: the Disintegration of Tribal Culture in the San Francisco Bay Area, 1769-1810. Menlo Park, California: Ballena Press, 1995.

Mock 1991 — Mock C.J. Historical Evidence of a Cold, Dry Summer During 1849 in the Northeastern Great Basin and Adjacent Rocky Mountains // Climatic Change. 1991. Vol. 18. P. 37-66.

NADA 2018 — North American Drought Atlas (NADA). 2018. URL: http://drought.memphis.edu/NADA/.

Palmer 1965 — Palmer W.C. Meteorological drought // U.S. Weather Bureau Research Paper. 1965. No. 45. P. 1-58.

Palóu 1926 — Palóu F. Historical Memoirs of New California by Francisco Palóu. Vol. 2. University of California Press, Berkeley, 1926.

Rowntree 1985 — Rowntree L.B. Drought During California's Mission Period, 1769-1834 // Journal of California and Great Basin Anthropology. 1985. Vol. 7 no. 1. P. 7-20.

Serra 1955a — Serra J. Writings of Junipero Serra. Vol. 1. Washington: Academy of American Franciscan History, 1955.

Serra 1955b — Serra J. Writings of Junípero Serra. Vol. 2. Academy of American Franciscan History, 1955.

Serra 1955c — Serra J. Writings of Junípero Serra. Vol. 3. Academy of American Franciscan History, 1955.

Serra 1955d — Serra J. Writings of Junípero Serra. Vol. 4. Academy of American

Franciscan History, 1955.

Schneider et al. 2012—Schneider T.D., Gonzalez S.L., Lightfoot K.G., Panich K.M., Russell M. a Land of Cultural Pluralism: Case Studies from California's Colonial Frontier // Contemporary Issues in California Archaeology. P. 319-337. Walnut Creek, California: Left Coast Press, Inc, 2012.

Smith et al. 2017—Smith E.M., Lucido J.A., Lydon S.E. FLORA, FAUNA, AND FOOD: Changing Dietary Patterns at the Spanish Royal, Presidio of Monterey, 1770-1848 // Boletín: Journal of the California Missions Foundation. 2017. Vol. 33 no. 1. P. 146-169.

Wahl et al. 2020—Wahl E.R., Hoell A., Zorita E., Gille E., Diaz H.F. a 450-Year Perspective on California Precipitation "Flips" // Journal of Climate. 2020. Vol. 33 issue 23. P. 10221-10237.

White 2019—White S. a comparison of drought information in early North American colonial documentary records and a high-resolution tree-ring-based reconstruction // Climate of the Past. 2019. Vol. 15. P. 1809–1824.

Williams 1993—Williams J.S. The Presidio of San Carlos de Monterey: the Evolution of the Fortress-Capital of Alta California. Tubac: the Center for Spanish Colonial Archaeology, 1993.

Wise, Dannenberg 2014—Wise E.K., Dannenberg M.P. Persistence of pressure patterns over North America and the North Pacific since AD 1500 // Nature Communications. 2014. Vol. 5, 4912.

WMO 2011—World Meteorological Organization (WMO). Guide to Climatological Practices (WMO-No. 100). 2011. URL: http://www.wmo.int/pages/prog/wcp/ccl/guide/documents/WMO_100_en.pdf.

Xianfeng et al. 2016—Xianfeng L., Xiufang Z., Yaozhong P., Shuangshuang L., Yanxu L., Yuqi M. Agricultural drought monitoring: Progress, challenges, and prospects // Journal of Geographical Sciences. 2016. Vol. 26 no. 6. P. 750-767.

Zhao, Dai 2015—Zhao T., Dai A. The Magnitude and Causes of Global Drought Changes in the Twenty-First Century under a Low–Moderate Emissions Scenario // Journal of Climate. 2015. Vol. 28. P. 4490-4512.

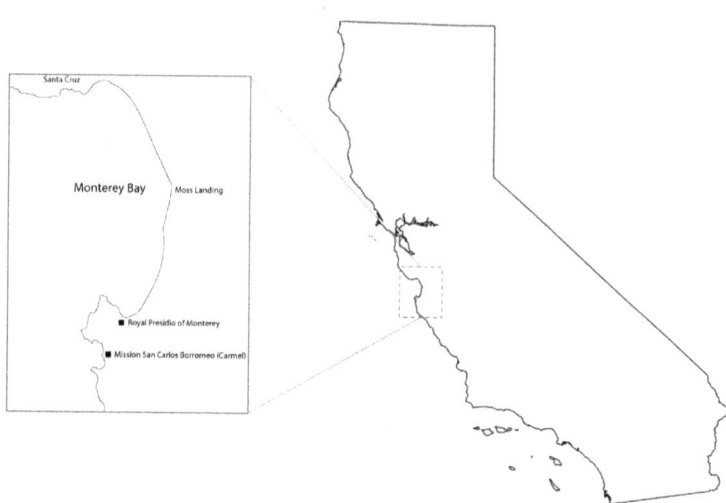

Figure 1. Map of California with detail of the Monterey Peninsula.

Source: Map of California outline by Babbage (2009). Retrieved from https://commons.wikimedia.org/wiki/File:Map_of_California_outline.svg. Map detail by Jennifer A. Lucido (2020).

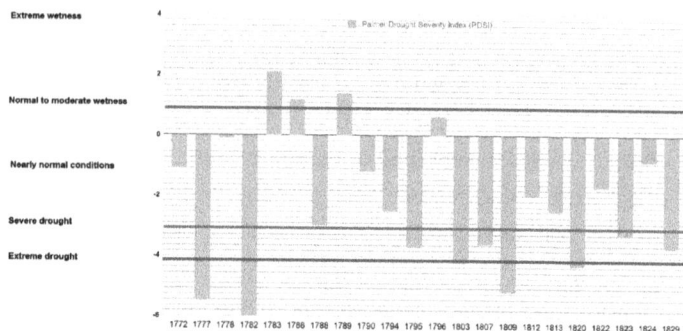

Figure 2. Dry Years in California from 1772-1829 based on PDSI

Source: PSDI data adapted from Meko, Stockton, and Boggess (1980) as cited in Rowntree (1985: 14). Graph by Jennifer A. Lucido (2020).

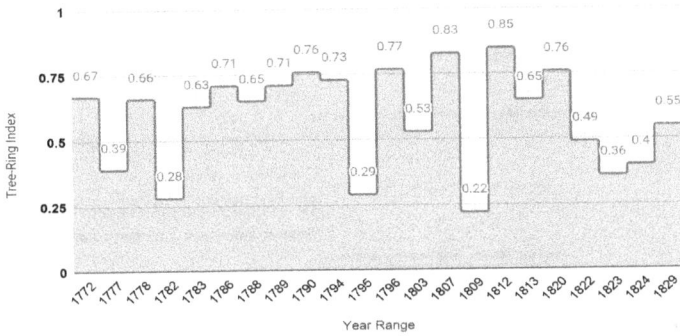

Figure 3. Tree-Ring Chronology of Dry Years in California from 1772-1829

Source: Tree-ring data adapted from Douglas (1976: 163) as cited in Rowntree (1985: 14). Graph by Jennifer A. Lucido (2020).

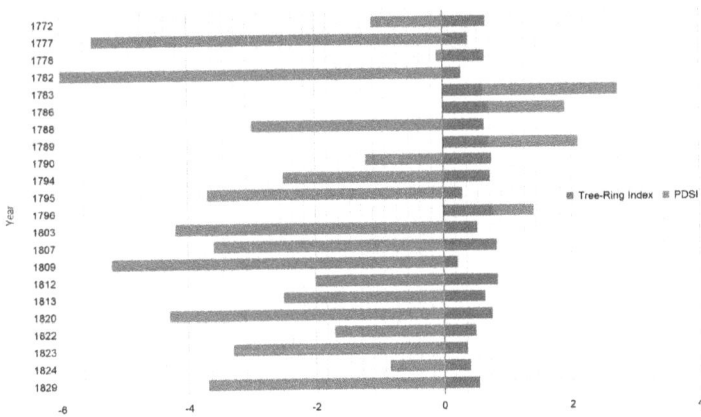

Figure 4. Comparison of Tree-Ring Chronology and PDSI Dry Years in California from 1772-1829

Source: Tree-ring and PDSI data adapted from Douglas (1976: 163) and Meko, Stockton, and Boggess (1980), as cited in Rowntree (1985: 14). Graph by Jennifer A. Lucido (2020).

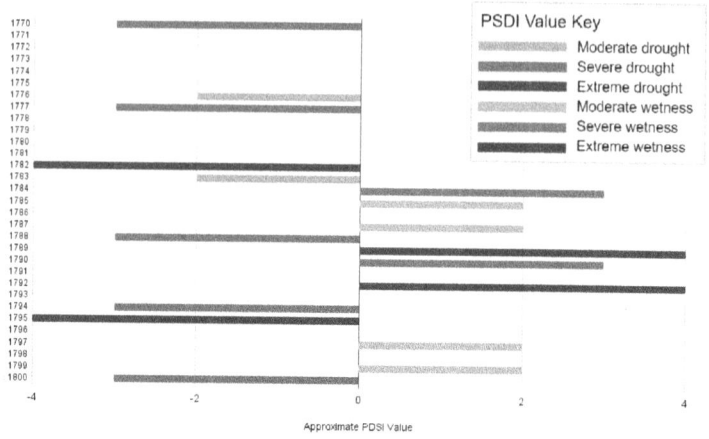

Figure 5. Reconstructed JJA PDSI 1770-1800 at Mission & Presidio of San Carlos and the broader Monterey Bay Area

Source: PDSI data adapted from North American Drought Atlas. 2018. Retrieved from: http://drought.memphis.edu/NADA/. PDSI value adapted from Dai & National Center for Atmospheric Research (2013). Retrieved from https://climatedataguide. ucar.edu/climate-data/palmer-drought-severity-index-pdsi. Graph by Jennifer A. Lucido (2020).

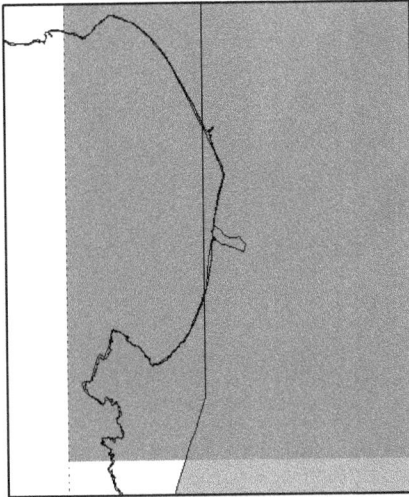

Reconstructed JJA PDSI 1770

1770

122W

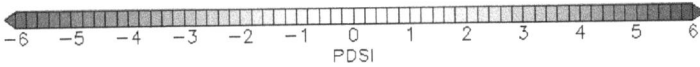

-6   -5   -4   -3   -2   -1   0   1   2   3   4   5   6
                              PDSI

Figure 6. Reconstructed JJA PDSI for the year of 1770 at Mission & Presidio of San Carlos and the broader Monterey Bay Area.

Source: North American Drought Atlas. 2018. Retrieved from: http://drought.memphis.edu/NADA

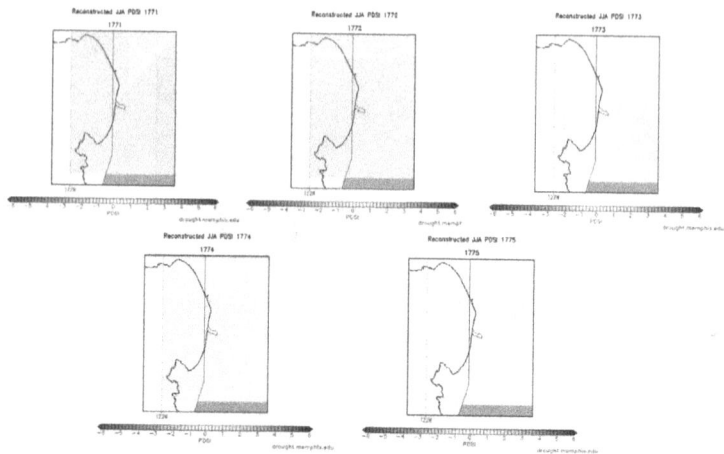

Figure 7. Reconstructed JJA PDSI for the years 1771-1775 at Mission & Presidio of San Carlos and the broader Monterey Bay Area.

Source: North American Drought Atlas. 2018. Retrieved from: http://drought.memphis. edu/NADA

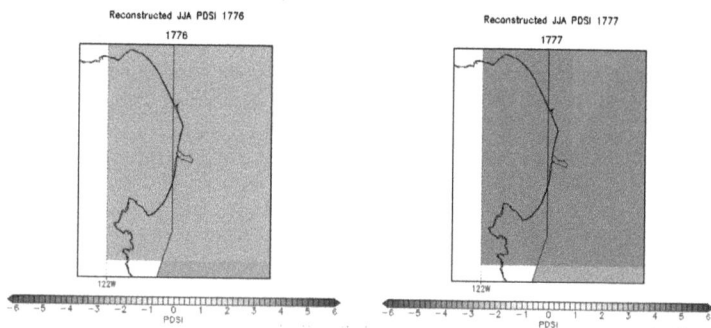

Figure 8. Reconstructed JJA PDSI for the years 1776 and 1777 at Mission & Presidio of San Carlos and the broader Monterey Bay Area.

Source: North American Drought Atlas. 2018. Retrieved from: http://drought.memphis. edu/NADA

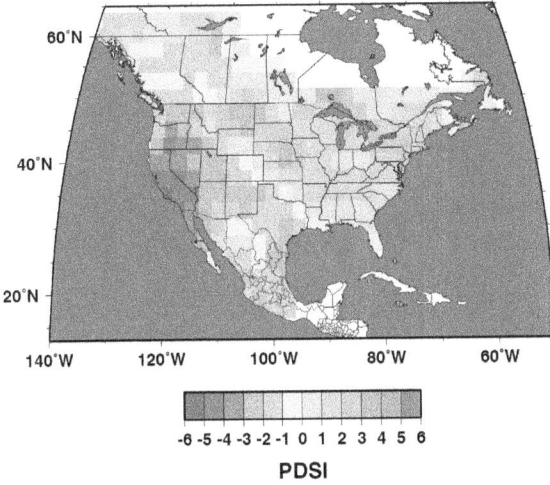

TREE-RING RECONSTRUCTED DROUGHT

1777

PDSI

Figure 9. Tree-ring reconstructed drought for the year of 1777 in the United States and Mexico.

Source: Cook and Krusic. 2004. Retrieved from: https://iridl.ldeo.columbia.edu/ SOURCES/.LDEO/.TRL/.NADA2004/.pdsi-atlas.html

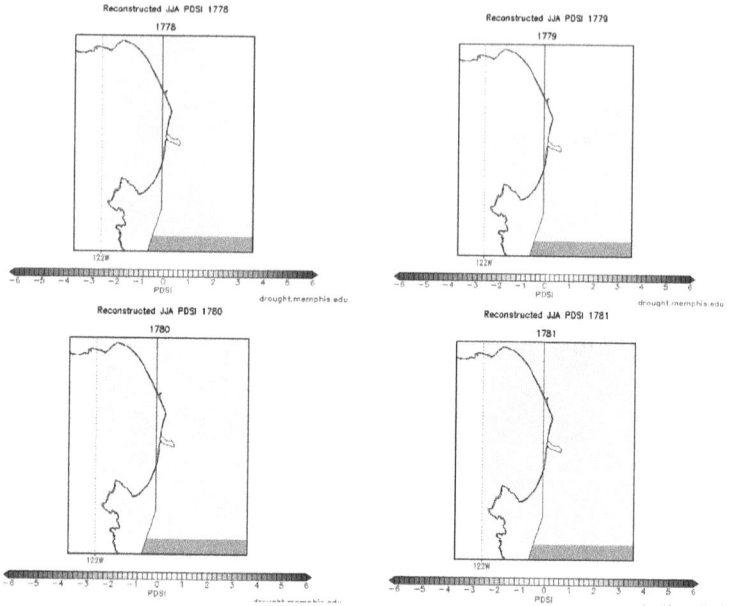

Figure 10. Reconstructed JJA PDSI for the yeas 1778-1781 at Mission & Presidio of San Carlos and the broader Monterey Bay Area.

Source: North American Drought Atlas. 2018Retrieved from: http://drought.memphis. edu/NADA

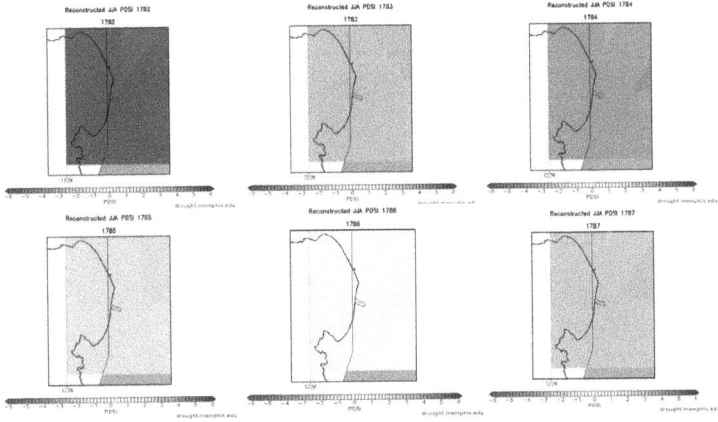

Figure 11. Reconstructed JJA PDSI for the years 1782-1787 at Mission & Presidio of San Carlos and the broader Monterey Bay Area.

Source: North American Drought Atlas. 2018. Retrieved from: http://drought.memphis.edu/NADA

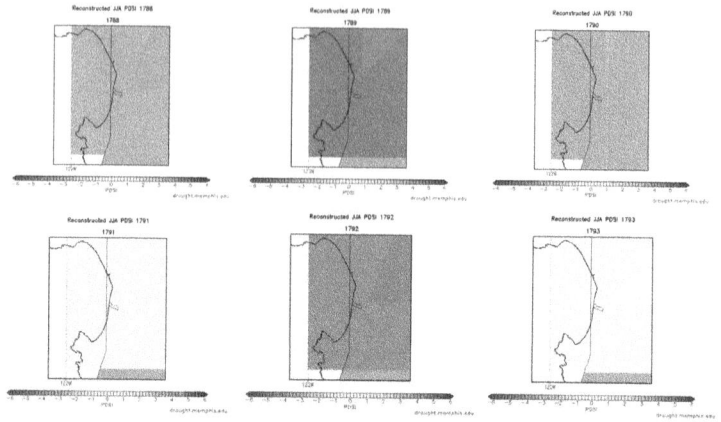

Figure 12 Reconstructed JJA PDSI for the year of 1788-1793 at Mission & Presidio of San Carlos and the broader Monterey Bay Area.

Source: North American Drought Atlas. 2018. Retrieved from: http://drought.memphis.edu/NADA

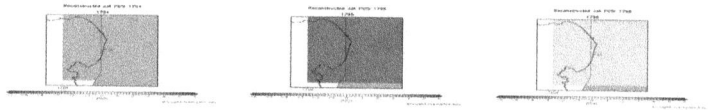

Figure 13 Reconstructed JJA PDSI for the year of 1794-1796 at Mission & Presidio of San Carlos and the broader Monterey Bay Area.

Source: North American Drought Atlas. 2018. Retrieved from: http://drought.memphis.edu/NADA

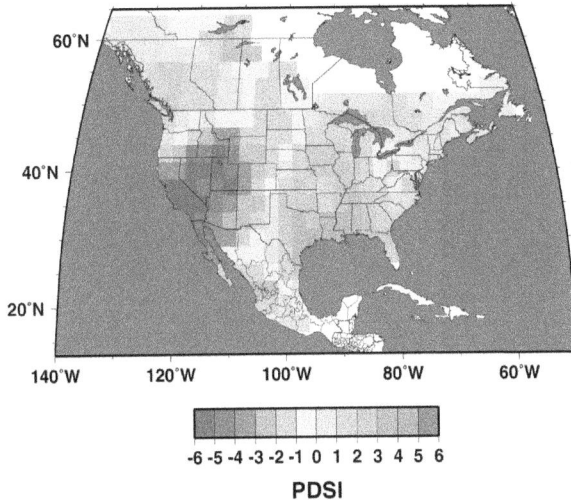

TREE-RING RECONSTRUCTED DROUGHT

1782

PDSI

Figure 14. Tree-ring reconstructed drought for the year of 1782 in the United States and Mexico.

Source: Cook and Krusic. 2004. Retrieved from: https://iridl.ldeo.columbia.edu/SOURCES/.LDEO/.TRL/.NADA2004/.pdsi-atlas.html

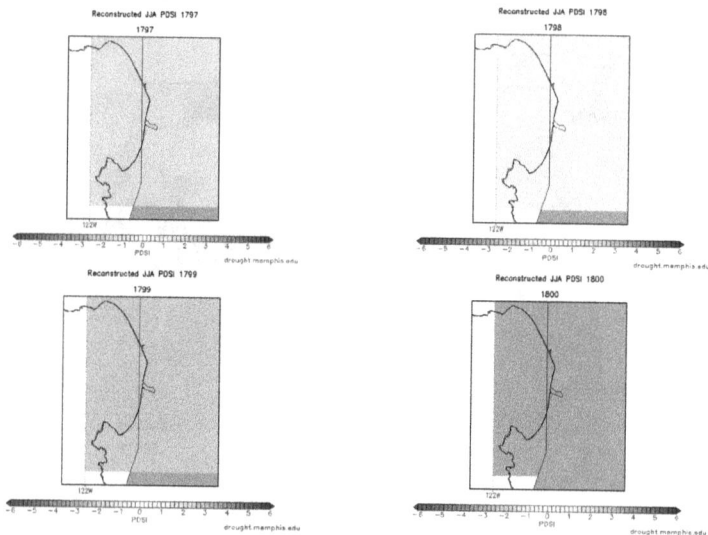

Figure 15. Reconstructed JJA PDSI for the years 1797-1800 at Mission & Presidio of San Carlos and the broader Monterey Bay Area.

Source: North American Drought Atlas. 2018. Retrieved from: http://drought.memphis. edu/NADA

Folk Magic and Folk Religion in Early New England

Gleb V. Aleksandrov

Introduction

Saying that early American colonial society was religious seems like a cliché, and for early New England doubly so. If an average person knows anything about early New England at all, they know it was founded by Puritans, and that Puritans were intensely, even fanatically, religious. One of the most common themes in historical scholarship is the influence of Puritan religiosity on social and political development of colonial and later American society (e.g. Breen 1970; Zakai 1986; Harrison 2005; Hall 2011).

That influence is hard to deny. Undoubtedly, many of the fundamental structures of colonial society were indeed heavily influenced by religion — the whole structure of the society first outlined in the Mayflower Compact was essentially a support system for a Separatist congregation. Later, the Bay Colony authorities paid close attention to religious affairs, to the point that some scholars have described Massachusetts as a theocracy (Zakai 1986). We don't completely share this view, but it is still quite widespread. Church membership was a major component of social status throughout New England, to the point that during the first years of the colonies it was sometimes a precondition to obtaining the coveted freeman status. Most foundational documents of the colonial era, including the Massachusetts Body of Liberties (which later had a significant influence on the US Constitution) were heavily influenced by the Scripture (Dreisbach 2019). The political thinking of New England elites was obviously heavily steeped in religion.

However, the influence of Puritan religiosity on other aspects of colonial life should not be overstated. While the first settlers in both Plymouth and Massachusetts were mostly members of specific congregations, neither colony was limited to those congregations. Even in Plymouth there were non-members of the congregation from the very start. As soon as the colonies began to grow the original religious unity was quickly disrupted. And, of course, even the most religious of Puritan divines were accompanied by servants and apprentices and distant relatives, many of whom were not nearly as fervent as their elders. As the colonies grew, the number of non-church members inevitably grew as well. Even the idea that the first building constructed in a new settlement was a meeting house, since people valued their religion so highly, holds true for Plymouth and Boston, but very few other settlements — in fact, there's evidence that many towns went without a church for years and years, if not decades, and while some of their inhabitants went to church in neighboring towns, many apparently were quite content without access to a church for extended periods of time. The number of full church members was always low. The percentage of extremely religious, extremely devout people compared to the general population of the colonies was in reality not that significant. While the notion of atheism is at best questionable when applied to early XVII century, most of the population even in mid-1630s Massachusetts was not as intensely religious as one might assume (Butler 1979).

The term Puritan, which we have used above to describe colonial religion, is technically a misnomer. The settlers of early New England belonged to several Calvinist denominations, and not all of them would agree to be described as Puritan—while Congregationalist and other Separatist congregations were certainly related, and recognized the fact, they were by no means "all Puritans", but rather a loose alliance of somewhat similar denominations, of which actual Puritans proper were a significant, but not a defining part. The differences between their versions of Calvinism were a subject of theological debates and analysis by many members of the colonial intellectual elites. More importantly for the purposes of this study, the very idea that people in the colonies belonged to certain specific denominations, each with its own, properly defined, dogma and ritual, that people chose what denomination they joined consciously, with full understanding of the differences, based on their own understanding of the Scripture is at best an oversimplification. Starting with the fact that the level of understanding of theology and even the Scripture among the colonists is often overestimated. The idea is that since reading the scripture is one of the cornerstones of the protestant doctrine which had a major influence on the protestant culture as a whole, of course "godly" colonists read it regularly and rigorously. The problem is that the evidence shows that at least in the XVIIth century that was not the case. As Jon Butler has demonstrated in his seminal and still influential article (Butler 1979) an average colonist in New England actually new very little about religion. Aside from maybe the Scrooby congregation, the original Plymouth Pilgrims of 1620, even the people who did consider themselves Puritans or Congregationalist or, later, Baptists, had very little idea of what distinguished all those branches of Christianity from one another. They understood the difference between Protestant and Catholic, but, aside from preachers and other learned men, even that was limited to very basic distinction between "popery" and everything else, based largely on superficial differences. Likewise, their knowledge of the Bible which some claim distinguished Protestant culture was at best limited.

Examining established churches and congregations and other manifestations of organized religion is certainly important, and there's no denying it's influence on the intellectual history of the colonies — again, religious elements in foundational documents and early narratives are extremely important and extremely prominent. But those documents and narratives were the product of the intellectual elites. Once we start addressing the spiritual life of an individual, religiosity as a part of the colonial experience, focusing on established organized religious traditions and movements becomes woefully inadequate, since for most colonists this organized and to a degree intellectualized religion was not nearly as familiar or as important as one might assume. We do, on the other hand, have ample evidence for widespread presence and importance of other spiritual practices, other modes of religious experience.

Religion, viewed from a human perspective, is at least in part a way for an individual to answer certain fundamental questions about their relationship with the world around them and the invisible forces outside of human control that govern it. in the case of the colonies the established dogma of Calvinism in any of its many flavors clearly didn't quite answer all those questions. The individual spiritual experience was certainly not limited to organized religion. And if we start thinking about the lasting influence of the colonial period on later American history, on the American worldview, it seems unwise to limit our exploration to just strict Protestant influences — other aspects of spiritual experience must have played a part as well, simply because they were so prominent and important for the colonists themselves.

What was, then, this spiritual undercurrent? What shaped the individual religious experience in addition to various established churches? the term "folk religion" seems appropriate as a description of that amalgamation of ideas, concepts and beliefs that existed outside organized religion but was no less important for the colonial mindset. The term "folk religion" is somewhat imprecise, and many definitions can be found in relevant scholarly literature. We find two of those definitions particularly useful and sufficient for our purposes. The first, compound, definition was suggested by Don Yoder several decades ago, but remains useful to this day. Yoder proposed five different possible definitions of folk religion. The first, evolutionary one, defined folk religion as the surviving elements of older forms of religion (in that context folk religion in Catholic Europe was seen as the survivals of pre-Christian religion and the folk religion in Protestant Europe as the survivals of Medieval Catholicism). The second definition identified folk religion as a mixture of official and "ethnic" religion, or rather of dominant religious tradition with subaltern ones (as happens for example in various American syncretic traditions which mix Christianity with Native American or African belief systems). The third, "folkloristic", definition implied "the interaction of belief, ritual, custom, and mythology in traditional societies", the fourth considered folk religion as the "folk interpretation and expression of religion". The final, and most useful in our opinion, despite its broadness, definition is a compound one, a combination of all four previous ones: "the totality of all those views and practices of religion that exist among the people apart from and alongside the strictly theological and liturgical forms of the official religion" (Yoder 1974). Or, as Matthias Zic Varul concisely put it "the relatively un-reflected aspect of ordinary practices and beliefs that are oriented towards, or productive of, something beyond the immediate here-and-now: everyday transcendence" (Varul, 2015). "Folk religion", if understood in this way, undoubtedly encompasses a range of practices which might otherwise be termed "folk magic" or "traditional healing" or "faith healing", all clearly covered by the above definition.

"Folk religion" in New England encompassed a wide range of beliefs and practices — it was a mixture of the traditional English folk magic practiced by the "cunning folk", remnants of folk Christianity prevalent before the reformation, some elements of alchemy and other learned traditions which inevitably trickled into wider "popular" culture. It is also important to note that such practices should not be dismissed as simply practical means of fixing certain everyday issues like treating diseases or making sure the beer brews properly. As Emma Wilby argues (convincingly, in our opinion), such practices always have a deeper, spiritual dimension, and clearly reflect a certain worldview, that does not entirely fit within the dominant Christian paradigm (Wilby 2005). The first purpose of this article is to examine these practices and beliefs in early New England. How did they manifest in everyday life and how did they influence the colonial mind? Secondly, we would attempt to trace the influence of folk religion on the later development of colonial culture and society. While this task is undoubtedly far too large to be accomplished within one article, we hope our examination will at the very least outline the potential areas for future research.

Witchcraft Trials, Confessions, and Folk Religion

The evidence for folk religion practices in colonial America is relatively widespread (see e.g. Demos 2004, Godbeer 1994). Early New England is something of an exception in this regard, because here the evidence is more limited, a lot of it confined to the materials related to witchcraft trials, the Salem case providing the most material. That does not necessarily mean that the practice itself was less widespread. Folk religion generally does not survive well in the historical record — in Europe, where it was incredibly widespread, the written sources prior to the creation of the first ethnographies, are mostly limited to witchcraft trial records as well. in New England there is an additional factor that changes the nature of the evidence available to us. The early colonial elites saw themselves as carrying out an important, even historical, mission, of establishing a godly society, and tried to present themselves and their history to the posterity accordingly. Similarly, in later American historical thinking the Pilgrims and the early Puritans occupied a prominent and defining place, their image being one of the cornerstones of American identity. This image was intentionally created and carefully maintained (see Butler 1979), so while it's doubtful any potential evidence of folk religion, such as semi-ethnographical "local histories" popular in the XIX century, was outright destroyed, it's very likely that it was intentionally not recorded to avoid distorting the established historical narrative. And, of course, some potentially useful evidence was indeed destroyed — parts of records and personal correspondence related to the Salem trials were destroyed by the families of the participants, mostly of the accusers. Of course, their intention was not to "cover up" the widespread use of folk magic among their relatives, but to hide their role in the trials which in just a few years after the events would be seen as a tragic and shameful episode (Norton 2002: 13). Still, one can't help but wonder what those destroyed papers could have told us about the spiritual life of ordinary colonists at the time. Despite that, the evidence is, while scarce compared to other colonies, still abundant. We will, however, primarily focus on the Salem case, since it provides us with several important detail which warrant further examination.

There are still several points of interest to us among the readily available and well-known documents related to the Salem witchcraft trials. The first is a clear reference to folk magic. in the early stages of the crisis Mary Sibley, a neighbor of the afflicted girls, directed Tituba, the Indian slave of Rev. Parris in making the so called "witch cake", a rather unpleasant concoction meant to protect the witchcraft victims. The purpose of that thing was not to harm the afflicted girls, but to prevent any further malicious influence on them, though the result was quite the opposite (Norton 2002: 20). What's notable here is firstly the ready availability of the recipe itself, clearly familiar to everyone involved. Secondly, it's notable that the episode happened fairly early on in the trials, so it was not some last desperate attempt to fix the situation that was getting out of control, but the first natural reaction of someone who wasn't even at that point directly involved in the events. Sibley was not an outsider, she was a proper Puritan, a member of Church. And yet her initial reaction was not to participate in a communal prayer, for example, which was done by the Rev. Parris himself (though that still is essentially a magical action). When questioned by other church members, she did repent after a detailed explanation of her sins, but it seems that without such an explanation traditional counter magic did not bother the pious woman at all (Ibid.). It was clearly a nearly-routine and quite natural action. When faced with perceived supernatural danger, the defense of choice was not prayer or calling the local minister (admittedly, the minister in question was far from popular among his parishioners and was at the center of a major controversy at the time), but a familiar and long-established folk magic recipe. Another similar instance of almost unconscious use of folk magic is the fortune-telling sessions conducted first by afflicted girls and later allegedly with the assistance of their father's slave Tituba, also involved in the witch-cake episode

(Breslaw 1996: 89-90). Unlike the making of the witch-cake, divination was, as one might expect, seen as sinful, and the guilt over participating in it likely played a part in exacerbating the "affliction" (if we consider it to be a genuine psycho-somatic phenomenon rather than an outright fabrication, but that seems to be a reasonable assumption). Nevertheless, the fact is that teenagers in a minister's household participated regularly in divinations. We know for a fact they did so with Tituba's assistance, but given how widespread such activities were in England, we have no real reason, other than our own ingrained ideas of super-religious Puritans, to assume those were the only occasions the girls in the Paris household engaged in similar harmless rituals, so widespread that they would likely be familiar not just to XVIIth century Englishmen, but to anyone today who ever hosted a slumber party as a teenager. The unusual part is the pronounced, sometimes overwhelming, sense of guilt experienced afterwards, inspire indeed by the Puritan religiosity. But that guilt did not stop the practice itself (and we can only guess if teenagers in other households, not minister's children, were affected by it in similar circumstances).

That internalized guilt is evident in one of the most puzzling aspects of the Salem story, the confessions. Why did so many people confess to being witches? And despite the abundant scholarship on the issue one thing is clear — there really isn't one single answer. For a while the prevalent theory was coercion. While outright physical torture was not used in Salem trials, emotional manipulation, scare tactics and peer pressure certainly all contributed to at least some confessions. However, the total number of confessions is large enough to cause doubt about whether that was the main reason. And of course, coercion does not explain voluntary confessions, when people who were not accused at all willingly came forward, or those accused of some minor infractions confessed to much greater ones. One reason that is rarely considered is the internalized guilt over the use of folk magic. The exploration of guilt is often tied to the idea that there were people who believed themselves to be witches and willingly performed certain rituals intending to harm others. However, feeling — and consequently admission — of guilt may have been born of entirely different source, the interaction between Puritan religiosity and traditional folk religion (Reis 2003).

The ministers both in England and in the colonies often preached against the use of "sorcery", divination, and other traditional magic practices. And devout puritans, including many church members in Salem, were very familiar with those harsh judgements of "witches". Which did not stop them from using all those traditional remedies, methods of divination and forms of supernatural protection. For a sufficiently religious person this contradiction, paired with even a cursory accusation, even a possibility of accusation, could cause severe stress — were they actually guilty? Yes, they perhaps did nothing to afflict the poor girls of Salem village, but they did once go to a wise woman to predict if their child will be born healthy, and they did ask the local "cunning man" to help find out who stole something... Everybody did. The number of confessions is in itself perhaps the most telling sign of how widely used folk magic was throughout New England. Salem became an exception because the circumstances allowed the internalized guilt to manifest itself in the form of confessions.

Folk magic, which may or may not be considered a part of folk religion. It does fit the definition we're using. No matter how unarticulated and how little reflected upon, the image of the world implied by the use of, for example, divination is certainly not completely confined by the official Calvinism. This worldview, which did not replace the one offered by organized religion, but supplemented it, can be glimpsed, albeit indirectly, through both confessions and interrogations conducted by Salem judges. There is a noticeable discrepancy between the imaginary worlds which the interrogators and the accused inhabited. The judges and interrogators were members of the colonial intellectual and social elite. When dealing with witchcraft they asked very specific questions which clearly reflected the "official" conception of witches and their evil – specifically, the connection with the Devil. The Puritan worldview was infused with supernatural forces, but one major principle was that God was the source of everything good, and the Devil of everything evil. For Puritans, the source of the evil they faced was the devil himself, and witches were merely his instruments. Consequently, the interrogators were far more interested in anything that had to do with the Devil, with meeting him, signing his black book, agreeing to do his bidding etc. And most confessors accommodated them, obligingly providing exactly the answers that were expected. This indirect (and probably unintended, at least not always intended) form of coercion was far from subtle, including the repetition of the same question in more and more detail, reducing it almost to a "yes or no" form (Briggs 1998; Norton 2002: 41–42; see in detail in: Breslaw 1996). The resulting picture of witchcraft in Salem village unsurprisingly conformed exactly to the expectations of the Puritan elites. The witches were in direct communication with the Devil himself, who guided them to commit all sorts of atrocities with the goal being the destruction of the godly community in America.

However, on those occasions the accused and the confessors were allowed to speak freely, their emphasis was rather different – they rarely mentioned the Devil at all. However, their narratives were full of recognizable motives, stressing the witches' connection to familiar spirits and the use of sympathetic magic. This discrepancy is well document for European witch trials by, for example, Robin Briggs (Briggs 1998), but little attention was given to it when applied to Salem. On closer inspection, however, it becomes quite obvious that the characteristically Puritan

"Devil narrative" is, much like in Europe, an artefact of elite culture inserted into decidedly archaic witchcraft story — so we can safely conclude that not just some rituals (like the witch-cake baking), but the general belief system associated with witchcraft and "cunning" was as alive and as widespread in 1690s New England as it was in late XVI century England or XV century France. If the New England colonies were more religious than the old England, it certainly didn't influence the general concept of the supernatural world as much as one might assume, though it did probably become an additional source of neurotic stress as evidenced by the voluntary confessions driven by internal sense of guilt.

Native Connections

One area where the ideas folk magic truly flourished in New England was the relations with Native Americans. a lot has been written about Puritan misconceptions of Native spirituality, but the main misconception that defined everything else is obvious. For the colonists the Indians were devil-worshippers, plain and simple. And of course, they used witchcraft — as befits the servants of the devil. The source of this notion is two-fold. Firstly, the Englishmen were ill equipped to understand the Native religions, and, crucially, had little interest in doing so. Several individuals had on occasion tried to argue that the Indians worship the same Creator as the Christians, though their religious practices are "corrupt" to some extent. But the consensus leaned heavily towards devil worship (Cave 1996: 13-47).

That solved several problems at once. Firstly, it allowed the colonists to disregard Native religion as legitimate out of hand and avoid the complexities of trying to understand it. Secondly, it justified the displacement of Native inhabitants of the colonies. If they religion was in some way "legitimate", that would mean they have to be dealt with as somewhat godly people, connected to the divine via a covenant similarly to the colonists themselves. However, if the Indians outright worshipped the Devil, they were by definition beneath such treatment.

Another reason for associating Indians with malevolent supernatural forces was the persistent connection between Native inhabitants of the New World and nature itself. From the earliest works discussing the potential settlement in the New World onwards, Indians were regularly described as "wild beasts of the woods" (Cave 1996: 16-18), as an inseparable part of the natural world. Indians were listed among the potential dangers the future colonists were going to face: storms, cold, hunger, Indians. The space outside the "civilized" areas was inherently unpredictable and dangerous, however the Puritan mindset did not allow for accidents. Everything that happened did so for a reason, guided by either divine or infernal powers. If the nature of the New World itself threatened the godly people of New England, it must have happened because of the Devil's attempts to destroy their community, perhaps with the assistance of his servants, the Indians. Another possible explanation, that a given disaster was a sign of divine anger or a call for renewing the communal commitment to godly way of life, was invoked almost as often, but in purely psychological terms the idea of devilish aggression was probably easier to accept.

In popular imagination the association of natural dangers with the Devil was less pronounced, however, it was influenced by persistent ideas about the relations between "wild" and occupied spaces characteristic of European culture in general. The forest, the wilderness beyond the occupied areas was a perpetual source of danger, both natural and supernatural. The "wild" space was outside human control, inhabited by dangerous entities of all kinds, from bandits and outcasts to malevolent spirits. in the New World this space was already inhabited.

The assumption that people who permanently live in that entirely un-humanized space are at the very least familiar with malevolent supernatural forces is, in this framework, logical. in the New World context, the Indians would have probably been associated with malevolent magic even if that served no purpose in justifying colonial expansion. There are other examples of colonial expansion where the indigenous population of a region became strongly associated with magic, especially malevolent magic, in the colonizing culture, such as Mari people in certain regions in Russia (Khristoforova 2011).

But the interpretation of Indian connection to malevolent magic shows the same discrepancy between the "official" concept, articulated by the intellectual elites, and the "folk" imagination we previously noted in relation to witchcraft. While the elites were more concerned with devil worship, once it came to actually articulating what the "witches" among the Indians were doing, their powers turned out to be essentially the same as those attributed to witches in English folklore. a great example here is Passaconaway, the great sachem of Pokanoket and a notoriously powerful sorcerer. His power was undeniable, no one among the colonists doubted the existence of this power. He could control the weather, make the trees dance, produce a live snake out of a dead snakeskin, create green leaves from ashes during winter as well as make himself invulnerable to weapons or cross great distances in a short time by flying (Cave 1996: 23; Wood 1977: 100-102). All classic abilities of a powerful witch from European folk tales, and none of them explicitly tied to the Devil. Much like in Europe, the Devil was primary a concern for religious and intellectual elites, while the imaginary world of the common folk was inhabited by lesser malevolent (and sometimes benevolent) entities, concerned with relatively down-to-earth, practical matters. And the threat they posed was not the existential threat to the soul, but a more immediate harm to health and property, requiring equally down-to-earth protection. While Puritan preachers were insistent that the only way to combat witchcraft, English or Indian, was through prayer and belief, colonial militiamen were not above using protective charms when dealing with Passaconaway. When dealing with native "powwows", for all the claims of the ultimate power of prayer, it seems for the colonists a good old fashioned rabbit's foot, or more likely a lucky coin, was still the method of choice. And there is indeed evidence of colonists employing these types of charms when dealing with the Indians, though it is rare — mostly because the majority of sources available to us were written by representatives of the more strictly Puritan elite culture. There is, however, ample evidence for the use of good fortune charms by soldiers during the Civil War and even World War I, and the evidence from XVII-XIX century Pennsylvania where such measures were widely used among the Pennsylvania Dutch, supposedly heavily Protestant ethnic group which practiced folk magic widely and openly (Yoder 1967; Yoder 1976; Kriebel 2007; Aleksandrov 2020).

That's not to say the Devil and the less immediate but more profound threat of divine punishment after death, threat to the soul not the body, were ignored by the majority of colonists. Folk religion rarely completely supplants the official doctrine even on the individual level, but it is preeminently concerned with everyday matters, offering solutions for far less profound but far more frequent problems. New England colonists successfully combined fervent Protestantism with a traditional view of the supernatural world filled with numerous heterogenous powers and entities, not necessarily confined to strict Protestant dichotomy of divine and infernal.

The association of magic with Native Americans did not stop there, in fact it was expanded to include other people of color. It's no coincidence that one of the first accused in Salem was Tituba, a Native servant of Samuel Parris (Breslaw 1996). Later, that persistent association would include the imagery connecting both Native and Black people to all kinds of occult practices. While intellectuals in XVIII and XIX centuries tended to dismiss these practices as "savage superstition", they certainly were real enough for the common folk (in the XVII century even the intellectual elites did not doubt the existence of, for example, Passaconaway's powers, they just had a very clear understanding of their origin from the Devil). Instead, the traditional apprehensiveness towards witchcraft and cunning would become one of the many reasons behind prejudice against people of color. We suspect that a closer examination of evidence specifically from the Southern colonies might reveal that the slave-owners still used the magical know-how of their slaves the same way they used the skills of the cunning folk back in England, though that is at this point just a strong suspicion. At the very least the connection between African-derived folk magic tradition and the unacknowledged folk spirituality in the South seems quite possible. While the emergence of syncretic religions such as voodoo was a complex process unrelated to the experience of the early English colonists, the prominent place such traditions occupy in American popular culture is partly explained by that association of the "other" with magic, a persistent feature of the American worldview since the earliest days of the colonies.

Folk Spirituality and Religious Revivals

Folk religion and official religion can and for the most part do coexist peacefully. But there is inherent tension between them. The presence of any alternative forms of spirituality is a challenge to the very idea of a dominant organized religion. The biggest challenge that draws the most attention is presented by other organized religions, and New England was no exception in this regard, the biggest opponents of ecclesiastical authorities were other denominations which, unlike folk religion, saw themselves as equally valid established churches. The Quakers, the Baptists, the Catholics, much later the Mormons were actively persecuted (Pestana 2009). Eventually all those became accepted modes of religious expression, becoming in turn part of the religious establishment, usually after making some concession in terms of either doctrine or practice to the then-dominant churches. Folk religion rarely becomes the focus of intentional persecution. Witchcraft trials can hardly be considered such because they are usually initiated not by the church authorities but by laymen. However, occasional confrontations can happen. Which brings us, indirectly, to the question of folk religion's influence on the colonial culture in general.

A key episode in the early history of Massachusetts was the Antinomian controversy, the conflict between the religious and secular authorities of the Bay Colony and a group of "heretics", whose theology differed from the Puritan orthodoxy in several important respects. a key figure among the "heretics" was Anne Hutchinson, whose trial and exile became the dramatic high point of the entire affair. The number of scholarly publications about the controversy in general and Hutchinson in particular, is staggering, so we will not go into any detail here, since extensive information on the situation can be found in a number of extremely impressive works (Bremer 1981; Huber 1985; Westerkamp 2021).

At first glance, the idea of associating Anne Hutchinson with folk religion seems strange. Hutchinson was notoriously well versed in Biblical and religious literature, and if anything, she might be considered a representative of the intellectual elite firmly tied to established religion. However, there are a few peculiar traits in her life as a religious leader that bear curious resemblance to traditional folk religion and even folk magic practices. We must clarify from the start that we do not in any way claim that Anne Hutchinson was a folk magic practitioner or anything of the sort. She was, indeed, a fervently Christian woman whose actual theological ideas were logical, if radical for the time, extensions of the Puritan doctrine. However, the way she functioned as a spiritual leader outside of the established church hierarchy in the social conditions of the time was to a degree influenced by the traditions of folk religion, simply because of the inevitable influence it had on everyday experience of people at the time.

The first part of Hutchinson's story that draws our attention is the social context of her early teaching. Hutchinson was a member of the church, who started to first advise others on matters of faith and eventually to promote her own teachings which aligned less and less with the Puritan orthodoxy. The first to receive her teachings were women whom she met in the course of her duties as a midwife. She assisted women during childbirth both physically and spiritually, eventually attracting a following significant enough to warrant separate gatherings to discuss religious matters. Later her teachings became so popular that separate gatherings for men became necessary, but the foundations were laid while she was still midwife first and foremost. We can only speculate if Hutchinson herself was consciously aware of that, but it's unlikely that her position itself had no influence on her growing spiritual authority. Midwives occupied a notable position in English folk culture at the time. They had access to specific, arcane knowledge, they were allowed into spaces where outsiders were usually not permitted. Their practice did naturally include magical elements, sometimes in the form of prayers, knowledge of which was also restricted. Unsurprisingly, midwives were often accused of being witches or served as the local "cunning women". in short, they wielded certain spiritual authority. Hutchinson, likely unintentionally, started her teaching in that position of authority, unrecognized officially, perhaps unrecognized consciously, but deeply ingrained in the cultural background.

In addition to being a midwife, Hutchinson often visited the sick, offering them spiritual assistance and likely praying together with them. This was also a traditional mode of action of cunning women, in fact their primary function. There is no evidence that Hutchinson consciously attempted faith healing or claimed to be able to heal, but when a midwife-turned-rising spiritual leader visits the sick and prays for them, and the sick get better (which some undoubtedly did), people familiar with and influenced by certain cultural patterns would draw conclusions. The fact that Hutchinson "used" prayers also fitted the pattern, by this point most of "spells" used by the cunning folk were in the form of prayers.

Anne Hutchinson did in fact claim powers that can be considered supernatural, specifically powers of prophecy and of what may be called a form of clairvoyance, specifically of being able to see the "elect", those destined to be saved in accordance with the Calvinist predestination doctrine, among the people. Both powers were not only anathema to Puritan divines but were exactly the kind of powers traditionally attributed to the cunning folk. Whether Anne Hutchinson wanted it or not, the formation of her authority in some respects followed the same pattern as the formation of the authority of the cunning folk. Interestingly enough, there is evidence that she was seen as such by the authorities she opposed. While never calling her a witch outright, John Winthrop summarized his feelings about Hutchinson's trial in a curiously suggestive fashion: "Thus it pleased the Lord to heare the prayers of his afflicted people [...] and by the care and indevour of the wise and faithfull ministers of the Churches, assisted by the Civill authority, to discover this Master-piece of the old Serpent" (Morgan 1981: 51). Not only there is a clear indication of connection with the Devil, essentially marking Hutchinson as something close to a witch, the very use of the word "afflicted" to describe the community disturbed by Hutchinson's teachings is reminiscent of the traditional way of describing those suffering from witchcraft.

Anne Hutchinson was the first spiritual leader of her kind in the New England colonies, but similar charismatic prophets heavily steeped in Christianity did appear throughout Europe and in England itself, and the ways they established their authority were equally suggestive of traditional, folklore patterns associated with magical practitioners, the cunning folk in the English cases. Later, of course, referencing such cultural patterns to establish authority was used consciously, for example in the political realm by Francois Duvalier in his attempts to establish an association between himself and certain figures in the vodou pantheon (Johnson 2006). It is impossible to believe that Anne Hutchinson was also using established cultural patterns to secure a position of authority for herself. But the situation itself clearly shows how deeply ingrained the influence of folk religion was in the colonies. The particulars changed in the New England context, but the pattern remained recognizable. Anne Hutchinson as a spiritual leader existed on the edge between the established and the unrecognized, in the ever-present interplay between organized and folk religion.

This mutual influence of folk religion and organized religion can be traced throughout American history. The early Quakers borrowed from folk magic "arsenal" extensively, if unconsciously (Butler 1979). Similarly, in the Pennsylvania folk magic tradition, successful powwows possessed recognizable spiritual authority. Since their success in healing and divination was tied to Christian beliefs, the more successful the magic was the godlier the practitioner was considered, to the point that some powwows were posthumously referred to as "saints" (even though the denominations prevalent in the region did not normally practice veneration of saints) (Aleksandrov 2020).

While a detailed exploration of these phenomena is outside of the scope of this article, it's worth noting that the spiritual leaders of the Great Awakening followed the same pattern as Anne Hutchinson. While the Old Lights based their spiritual authority on education, biblical interpretation and so on, much like Puritan authorities in Massachusetts, the New Lights emphasized personal spiritual experience, and often supplemented it with "divine" supernatural abilities, including prophetic visions and faith healing—patterned essentially after folk magic. This is even more evident in contemporary megachurches which combine the structure and authority of organized religion with the entire range of magical practices, from healing to exorcism and divination, lifted directly from folk magic. in Catholicism and larger Protestant denominations such practices were always looked down upon and have slowly phased out of official recognition, further dividing organized and folk religion. American mega-churches, on the other hand, can be considered a form of organized religion which co-opted a number of practices from folk religion to ensure wider popular appeal, proving in the process how important that folk religion was and still is for large portions of the population. Normally, folk religion lacks that organizational power and direct authority, leaving the larger spiritual issues to organized religion, but in the mega-church case it usurps both functions, providing both everyday remedies for everyday spiritual problems and the fundamental answers to fundamental questions about the relations between a person and the uncontrollable forces outside their control. The confrontation between folk religion and organized religion which manifested both in the story of Anne Hutchinson and in the interplay of the official Devil narrative and folk beliefs in Salem witchcraft trials remained a crucial part of the American spiritual experience.

Conclusion

Even with the available evidence limited due to many factors, including conscious interference of colonial elites trying to present the society they were writing about as more "godly" and more pious than it really was, it's obvious that folk religion was still a major part of colonial life even in early New England. It's presence is clearly visible, even outside the personal narratives, in the discrepancy between "official" and "folk" interpretations of witchcraft, both during the Salem trials and in dealing with Native American spirituality. More importantly, as we have shown, folk religion was so deeply engrained in the culture of New England colonists, that it had influenced the development of organized religion to an extent. Anne Hutchinson, probably the most charismatic spiritual leader in early Bay Colony and the center of the Antinomian controversy, was, of course, a Christian first and foremost. However, the way her spiritual authority was formed and functioned was in many ways similar to the authority of a traditional folk magic practitioner. Similar interactions between established and folk religion can be seen, for example, among the Pennsylvania Dutch in later colonial period.

More importantly, a similar pattern can be observed in later and even contemporary religious revivals. The contemporary mega-churches, for example, employ many of the methods and techniques of folk religion. They rely on charismatic leaders, whose authority is based on claims of personal spiritual experience, rather than learning and refined theological thought. The powers such leaders claim, such as faith healing and prophecy, are broadly similar to those of the cunning folk. Such churches tend to combine the roles of both folk religion and organized religion, providing both tangible, practical solutions to everyday problems (usually the domain of folk religion) and answers to more fundamental spiritual issues (the purview of organized religion). While in Europe established religion and various folk practices grew more and more separate as time went on, folk spirituality finding little support from religious organizations, in America they grew closer, providing the organized religion with influence on everyday activity in all spheres of life it usually does not possess, and endowing folk religion with organizational power, structure and influence it normally lacks. At the same time, the practices remained essentially the same as in folk religion, and were underlined by a relatively underdeveloped explanatory model, as folk religion often is, so it wasn't the case of a new organized religion growing out of folk beliefs.

The reason for this peculiar transformation was, we believe, the colonial experience itself. The background was the same, folk religion in early New England consisted of the same beliefs and practices as in England. Its influence on everyday life may have been more prominent in the colonies, due to the enhanced sense of threat from the environment experienced by the colonists, especially in the early years of the settlement. However, the authority of any established church in the colonies was never as extensive as in England. Even in early Massachusetts with its dominating Puritanism, the established church did not have nearly as much organized political power at its disposal as in England. And crucially, the colonies afforded those unhappy with the domination of a particular denomination a relatively simple way out, voluntary exile and settlement somewhere beyond the borders of established authority. This was exactly the way Anne Hutchinson's followers took, relocating to Rhode Island. in short, the fragmented nature of religious authority in the colonies, split between multiple denominations and individual congregations, did not allow the organized religion to distance itself from folk religion as effectively as it was done in Europe. As a result, folk religion became an even more prominent part of spiritual life in the colonies, eventually partly merging with organized religion. It's influence on all aspects of American worldview should not be dismissed. From this point of view, the magical practices of contemporary megachurches, the ever-present popularity of psychics of all sorts, the periodical waves of increased interest in the occult, the proliferation of syncretic religions, are not some rudiments of archaic believes suddenly manifesting in the modern age, but an inherent and ever-present part of American spiritual life, its important constituent part. Evolving and acquiring new features throughout time, often under some outside influence, it grows naturally from the importance of folk religion in early modern society, which, in the colonial context, was not suppressed or ignored, but flourished, influencing the organized religion and the society as a whole more prominently than in the Old World. Its influence on other aspects of society and its development is still to be explored.

References

Aleksandrov 2020 — Aleksandrov G. «The Long-Lost Friend»: the witchcraft and healing among Pennsylvanian Germans in the 20th and 21st centuries // in Umbra. Demonology as a Semiotic System. Vol. 9. Moscow: Russian State University for Humanities, 2020.

Breen 1970 — Breen T. The Character of the Good Ruler: a Study of Puritan Political Ideas in New England, 1630-1730. New Haven: Yale University Press, 1970.

Bremer 1981 — Bremer F. Anne Hutchinson, Troubler of the Puritan Zion. Huntington, New York: Robert E. Krieger Publishing Company, 1981.

Breslaw 1996 — Breslaw E. Tituba, the Reluctant Witch of Salem. N.Y., London: New York University Press, 1996.

Briggs 2002 — Briggs R. Witches and Neighbours: the Social and Cultural Context of European Witchcraft. N.Y.: Penguin, 1998.

Butler 1979 — Butler J. Magic, Astrology, and the Early American Religious Heritage,

1600-1760 // the American Historical Review. 1979. Vol. 84 (2). P. 317-346.

Cave 1996 — Cave A. The Pequot War. Amherst, Boston: University of Massachusetts Press, 1996.

Demos 2004 — Demos J. Entertaining Satan: Witchcraft and the Culture of Early New England. Oxford, N.Y.: Oxford University Press, 2004.

Dreisbach 2019 — Dreisbach D. Introduction: Christianity and American Law // Great Christina Jurists in American History. Cambridge: Cambridge University press, 2019. P.1-15.

Godbeer 1994 — Godbeer R. The Devil's Dominion: Magic and Religion in Early New England. Cambridge: Cambridge University Press, 1994.

Hall 2011 — Hall D. a Reforming People: Puritanism and the Transformation of Public Life in New England. Chapel Hill: University of North Carolina Press, 2011.

Harrison 2005 — Harrison P. 'Fill the Earth and Subdue It': Biblical Warrants for Colonization in Seventeenth-century England // Journal of Religious History. 2005. Vol. 29. P. 3-24.

Huber 1985 — Huber E. Women and the Authority of Inspiration: a Re-examination of Two Movements from a Contemporary Feminist Perspective. Lantham: University Press of America, 1985.

Johnson 2006 — Johnson P. Secretism and the Apotheosis of Duvalier // Journal of the American Academy of Religion. 2006. Vol. 74 №2. P. 420-445.

Khristoforova 2011 — Khristoforova O. Witches and Victims: Anthropology of Sorcery in Contemporary Russia. Moscow: OGI, 2011. [In Russian]

Kriebel 2007 — Kriebel D.W. Powwowing Among the Pennsylvania Dutch: a Traditional Medical Practice in the Modern World. University Park: Pennsylvania State University Press, 2007.

Morgan 1981 — Morgan E. The Case Against Anne Hutchinson // Anne Hutchinson: Troubler of the Puritan Zion. Huntington, New York: Robert E. Krieger Publishing Company, 1981. P. 51–57.

Norton 2002 — Norton M.B. in the Devil's Snare: the Salem Witchcraft Crisis Of 1692. N.Y.: Vintage Books, 2002.

Pestana 2009 — Pestana C.G. Quakers and Baptists in Colonial Massachusetts. Cambridge: Cambridge University Press, 2009.

Reis 2003 — Reis E. Confess or Deny? What's a "Witch" to Do? // OAH Magazine of History. 2003. Vol. 17 (4). P. 11-16.

Varul 2015 — Varul M. Consumerism as Folk Religion: Transcendence, Probation and Dissatisfaction with Capitalism // Studies in Christian Ethics. 2015. Vol. 28 (4). P. 447-460.

Westerkamp 2021 — Westerkamp M. The Passion of Anne Hutchinson: An Extraordinary Woman, the Puritan Patriarchs, and the World They Made and Lost. New York: Oxford University Press, 2021.

Wilby 2005 — Wilby E. Cunning Folk and Familiar Spirits: Shamanistic Visionary Traditions in Early Modern British Witchcraft and Magic. Brighton, Portland: Sussex Academic Press, 2005.

Wood 1977 — Wood W. New England's Prospect (1634). Amherst: University of Massachusetts Press. 1977.

Yoder 1967 — Yoder D. Twenty Questions on Powwowing // Pennsylvania Folklife. 1967. Vol. 17. No. 4.

Yoder 1974 — Yoder D. Toward a Definition of Folk Religion // Western Folklore. 1974. Vol. 33 (1). P. 1-15.

Yoder 1976 — Yoder D. Hohman and Romanus: Origins and Diffusion of the Pennsylvania German Powwow Manual // American Folk Medicine: a Symposium. Berkeley: University of California Press, 1976.

Zakai 1986 — Zakai A. Theocracy in New England: the Nature and Meaning of the Hole Experiment in the Wilderness // Journal of Religious History. 1986. Vol. 14 (2). P. 133-151.

Sifting Through the Debris Once More: Lessons from the United States' Civil War

J. Edward Lee

More books have been written about the American Civil War than any other event in our nation's history. The shelves of my university's library groan with Gettysburg, sob with the shame of slavery, chronicle the contributions of spies, analyze military maneuvers, and tell us of heroism, cowardice, mistakes, triumph, strategy, and defeat. What more can be written or said about this epic war, its causes, its participants, its meaning, and its aftermath?

I suggest that sifting through the debris of a conflict which resulted in the deaths of 750,000 Americans and pondering the wreckage left by four years of ferocious fighting still can be useful. There are lessons which can yet be learned which might be applicable beyond America's borders. These lessons are essential in the world of the 21st Century, a world of conflict, ethnic tensions, territorial ambitions, economic rivalry, and demonstrations of senseless cruelty.

The American Civil War did not just erupt in December 1860 when South Carolina seceded from the Union. The sections, North and South, were destined to clash from the start. The North's economy was based on manufacturing and finance. The South was tied to agriculture, primarily the cultivation of cotton. At the heart of this inevitable war was slavery. Human bondage arrived in Jamestown, Virginia in the early 1600s. in South Carolina, slave markets opened from the beginning: 1670. Slavery was an emotional, economic, political catalyst that lit the fire of conflict long before 1860. It was, indeed, as historian Kenneth Stampp reminds us, "the peculiar institution," and the addiction of slavery would rip America apart. By 1860, everyone had reached an opinion about slavery. The South's leadership was increasingly defensive about it while Abolitionists created in 1854 the Republican Party, an emerging movement of people hostile to expansion of "the peculiar institution."

We need to face the reality that people owning other people, dominating their lives, is morally wrong for any reason. Skin color does not connote inferiority. No ethnic group is superior to another. No government should economically control a minority population. These are essential, universal truths. "All men are created equal," as Thomas Jefferson proclaimed in 1776, means *all* men and *all* women. No one can be excluded for any reason from "inalienable rights": life, liberty, and the pursuit of happiness. Differences among humans should not generate battlefield conflict but should foster genuine ethnic acceptance. The American Civil War settled this matter permanently: *no one can own anyone else.*

There are those who argue the Civil War was about states' rights. They miss the essential point made in the preceding paragraph. States have no right to endorse inequality. The Unite States Constitution's Tenth Amendment does give powers to the respective states, but these do not include robbing humans of dignity and freedom. We fought a costly war over that constitutional point with battles such as Gettysburg, Antietam, and the Wilderness. But, after the dead were buried and the wounded hobbled away, the indisputable fact remains: states are part of a permanent Federal Union, limited in their authority, and *cannot secede.*

The Civil War's ultimate outcome should have been understood from the beginning by North and South. The North manufactures and equipped its troops with weapons and uniforms. The South could not smuggle manufactured products past the Union blockade. As the war progressed, the Confederates ran out of everything from weapons to shoes. There were food riots in Richmond, Virginia. Shortages, no foreign friends waiting on southern cotton because it was tainted by "the peculiar institution," no recognizable currency, a chaotic rail system which impeded troop movement, closed harbor cities like Charleston, clashes along the Mississippi River, a huge population disparity of 23,000,000 northerners compared to 9,000,000 southerners (of whom 4,500,000 were enslaved people), coalesced to give the North a tremendous edge throughout the war. All these factors determined the war's outcome long before 1865 and the surrender of General Robert E. Lee to General Ulysses S. Grant at Appomattox Court House.

After the 1865 surrender, the Civil War continued in a different uniform and on re-designed battlefields. The terrorist organizations, the Ku Klux Klan and the Knights of the White Camellia, impeded reconstruction and national healing from 1865 until 1877. Daylight in the South belonged to occupying Union troops and the freed men and freed women. As the sun set, however, ex-Confederates like Dr. Rufus Bratton of South Carolina transformed themselves into tormentors of the formerly enslaved people, roaming the countryside and inflicting fear and pain. As Margaret Mitchell said in 1936 when her best-selling novel *Gone*

With the Wind was published, "I grew up in an conquered land." That is the way Dr. Bratton and his allies viewed the South after Appomattox. It was only a matter of time before the Union troops withdrew from the "conquered land" and racial distinctions morphed into Jim Crow laws. The American South, we should note, changes slowly and racism (or ethnic hatred) often goes dormant until it rises in the next season. I suggest that this is not a uniquely American phenomenon.

So, what do we gain by sorting through the Civil War's debris? We benefit from understanding the evils of slavery and racism, the inability to rupture the Federal Union through state secession, the stupidity of war when outnumbered and out-supplied, and the obstacles to successful and lasting reconstruction. Those are lessons that speak to us beyond the carnage of 1861-1865 and beyond the borders of my own country.

His Truth is Marching On: Capt. James Williams and the Ku Klux Crisis in Reconstruction York County

Zachary A. Lemhouse

The Reconstruction Era is a period of rebuilding the United States socially, politically, and economically. It is typically defined as occurring between 1865 and 1877. Plans to admit the former Confederate States back into the Union were developed and promoted by President Abraham Lincoln, President Andrew Johnson, and the Republican controlled congress of the United States. Lincoln's plan for Reconstruction, which he started developing before the end of the war, was designed to easily integrate the former Confederate States back into the Union. Lincoln's ten percent policy required a meager ten percent of a state's voting population to swear allegiance to the Union before they could reconstitute their state government and send representatives to Congress.* However, Lincolns plan for reconstruction died with him on April 14, 1865. President Johnson's plan for Reconstruction was similar to Lincoln's plan. Under Johnson's plan, former Confederate States were still required to adhere to the ten percent policy as well as ratify the Thirteenth Amendment to the United States Constitution. in addition, Johnson required southern elite, anyone with $20,000 worth of property or more, to individually request a presidential pardon in order to retain their property.**

Andrew Johnson's plan for Reconstruction would remain in effect until his impeachment in 1867. Though Johnson was not removed from office, his power as President was significantly curtailed. The Radical Republicans in Congress took this opportunity to institute their own Reconstruction policy. Congress' plan for Reconstruction split the South into five military districts. South Carolina was in the second military district. Each district was occupied by United States troops with the hope that they would keep order and enforce the Thirteenth, Fourteenth, and Fifteenth Amendments.***

The South would be forever changed as a result of Reconstruction. The Thirteenth Amendment to the United States Constitution freed four million people when it outlawed the institution of slavery. Slavery, which had dominated southern economics since the colonial era, was replaced with a different form of labor known as sharecropping. Faced with few other options for making a living, sharecropping gave Freedmen the means to live on separate tracts of land and raise crops. in exchange for working the land, a share of the crop was owed to the landowner each year.

* Foner, Eric. a Short History of Reconstruction: 1863-1877 (New York: Harper Collins Publishers, 1990), 16-17.

** Ibid, 82-85.

*** Foner, Eric. a Short History of Reconstruction: 1863-1877 (New York: Harper Collins Publishers, 1990) 122-123.

Generally, sharecroppers kept between one-third to one-half of the year's crop depending on whether the landowner provided the tools, fertilizer, and seed.* However, if the land failed to yield a good harvest, a sharecropper might not earn enough to pay his debts to the landowner. Sharecropping often created a cycle of debt that kept African American families economically dependent on the South's old planter class. Many African Americans could not read or write, making them targets for unscrupulous business dealings, being charged exorbitant prices for goods, and higher interest rates. a few sharecroppers were eventually able to purchase land of their own, such as Greene and Malinda Bratton who were formerly enslaved on the Bratton Plantation.**

Many Whites saw sharecropping as an opportunity to reestablish dominance. Led by Mississippi and South Carolina, Southern states passed laws, called Black Codes, which limited the rights of Freedmen and prevented them from achieving political and economic autonomy. One law required every black adult to sign a yearly labor contract with a white person. Those who refused risked prosecution under state law. Black Codes and widespread violence against Freedmen provoked a flurry of protest from Radical Republicans who championed legislation that repealed nearly every Black Code by 1868. Despite their efforts, racial discrimination and violence persisted.***

The Thirteenth Amendment was followed by the Fourteenth and Fifteenth Amendments to the Constitution. The Civil Rights

* Foner, Eric. *a Short History of Reconstruction: 1863-1877* (New York: Harper Collins Publishers, 1990) 79.

** Ayers, Edward L., et al., *American Passages: a History of the United States* (Fort Worth, TX: Harcourt, 2000), 1:518-21; Green Bratton sharecropping agreement. Bratton Family Paper Collection, South Caroliniana Library, University of South Carolina, Columbia, SC.

*** *Reconstruction: America After the Civil War,* Tony Rossi/Henry Louis Gates, Jr (Washington, DC: McGee Media & Inkwell Films, 2019); Foner, Eric. *a Short History of Reconstruction: 1863-1877* (New York: Harper Collins Publishers, 1990) 93-95

Act of 1866 and the Fourteenth Amendment (1868) granted citizenship to African Americans while the Reconstruction Acts (1867) and the Fifteenth Amendment (1869), provided the right to vote to African American men. Whites, who had long held power over African Americans, saw their power diminish. This loss of power coupled with their "dissociation from the emerging society" led to anger that manifested itself in racial violence perpetrated by vigilante groups like the Ku Klux.[*]

This secret organization originated in Pulaski, Tennessee in 1866. They came to York County in 1868. The Ku Klux was supported by Whites sympathetic to white supremacy in the South. Wearing masks to hide their identities, Ku Klux members waged an underground campaign of terror and violence directed at anyone (white or black) in Republican leadership and those who defended civil rights for African Americans.[**] South Carolina's Governor, Robert Kingston Scott, elected in 1868, publicly condemned the violent actions of the Ku Klux. He pressured Wade Hampton III, former Confederate general and leader of the Democratic State Committee, to do the same. in October 1868, Hampton addressed the state's Democrats calling for an end to violence.[***]

Though violence had been temporarily suppressed, intimidation by the Klan still had a disastrous impact on the local African American community, particularly when it came to African American suffrage. Because ballots of the time were visibly marked, it was obvious as to which party a voter supported. Anyone supporting the Republican Party was a potential target

[*] West, Jerry L. *The Reconstruction Ku Klux Klan in York County South Carolina 1865–1877* (Jefferson, NC: McFarland & Company Inc., 2002), 3.

[**] Foner, Eric. *a Short History of Reconstruction: 1863-1877* (New York: Harper Collins Publishers, 1990) 146.

[***] Hampton, Wade, et al. "To the People of South Carolina," *Edgefield Advertiser*, (Edgefield, SC: Nov 4, 1868); West, Jerry L. *The Reconstruction Ku Klux Klan in York County South Carolina 1865-1877* (Jefferson, NC: McFarland & Company Inc., 2002) 47.

of the Ku Klux. At one polling station in York County, several men "having no official capacity" recorded the names of every person that voted Republican. Members of the African American community were so fearful of reprisal from the Klan that some refused to leave their homes on Election Day.[*]

In an attempt to embolden African American voters in South Carolina, Governor Scott signed a bill into law on March 16, 1869 that made all men (black or white) between the ages of 18 and 45 eligible for paid militia service. Three militia units were raised in York County as a result of the Governor's legislation: one in the Cherokee Township, one in Rock Hill, and the third near Forest Hall, the home of John S. Bratton, Jr. and his wife Harriet Jane Rainey Bratton. James Williams, a freedman formerly enslaved on the Bratton Plantation, enlisted in the Forest Hall militia and was eventually appointed captain.[**]

Initially, the militias were integrated but white militiamen resigned. The absence of Whites left holes that were filled by African Americans. When the Governor's office refused to raise exclusively-white militias, anger amongst Whites flared. The exclusively-black militias triggered an "arms race" as fearful Whites acquired weapons with which to "protect themselves" from black militiamen.[***]

When Governor Scott realized that the militias formed with his legislation were exacerbating tensions in the community, he disbanded them at the end of January 1871. Despite these efforts, violence in York County continued to grow. Attacks peaked

* West, Jerry L. *The Reconstruction Ku Klux Klan in York County South Carolina 1865–1877* (Jefferson, NC: McFarland & Company Inc., 2002) 48

** West, Jerry L. *The Reconstruction Ku Klux Klan in York County South Carolina 1865–1877.* McFarland & Company Inc. Jefferson, North Carolina. 2002. 47; Trelease, Allen W. *White Terror: the Ku Klux Klan Conspiracy and Southern Reconstruction* (New York, NY. Harper & Row, Publishers, 1971) 365.

*** West, Jerry L. *The Reconstruction Ku Klux Klan in York County South Carolina 1865–1877.* McFarland & Company Inc. Jefferson, North Carolina. 2002. 47–48 during the state elections in the fall of 1870 and continued into 1871 with a reported 11 murders and 600 beatings in York County alone. Capt. James Williams understood that the state-established militias were the only protection freedmen truly had from the nightly raids perpetrated by the Ku Klux. Therefore, he refused to disarm and disband and, in doing so, attracted the attention of the local Ku Klux.*

James Williams was well known to York County Ku Klux. He regularly spoke openly against Ku Klux atrocities and was accused by local whites of making threats to "kill from cradle to grave" should attacks on African Americans not cease. Others accused Williams and his militia of arson.** James Williams was brought further into the public eye when he used his authority as militia captain to arrest a white man named Robert Mendenhall who had started an altercation with one of Williams's militiamen.***

In an attempt to reduce the growing tension, local African American leader and preacher, Elias Hill, organized a public meeting near his home in Clay Hill on February 11, 1871. Both white and African American leaders were present, including James Williams. According to a report of the meeting published in the *Yorkville Enquirer* on February 16, 1871 "all acts of violence were heartily condemned."**** Despite this condemnation, Ku Klux violence continued. On the afternoon of March 6, Williams gave an impassioned speech on the steps of the Rose Hotel in which he once again openly condemned the actions of the Ku Klux. This public condemnation coupled with Williams' refusal to disband and disarm enraged the Ku Klux. The following

* Farris, Scott. *Freedom on Trial: the Defeat and Demise of the Post Civil War Ku Klux Klan* (Guilford, Connecticut: Lyons Press, 2020) 33.

** West, Jerry L. *The Reconstruction Ku Klux Klan in York County South Carolina 1865-1877.* McFarland & Company Inc. Jefferson, North Carolina. 2002. 70–71.

*** "The Trial of the Ku Klux," *Yorkville Enquirer* (York, SC: December 21, 1871) 3

**** "Public Meeting at Clay Hill." *Yorkville Enquirer.* York, South Carolina. February 16, 1871 morning, on March 7, 1871, Ku Klux raided Williams's home and lynched him in retaliation. Miles S. Carroll, a Ku Klux present the night of James Williams' murder, recounted that,

We proceeded on foot to the house [of James Williams] and knocked on the door... when we asked where Jim was his wife said she did not know... We made a thorough search of the house but did not find him. Dr. Bratton told someone to pull up some of the plank flooring... and sure enough, there was Jim crouched down under the floor. We hauled him out and placed a rope around his neck... when someone spied a large tree with a limb running out 10 or 12 feet from the ground... We left Captain Williams dangling from that limb.*

Later that day, the York County Coroner conducted an in-quest into Williams's murder at the Brattonsville Store located in the Brick House.** the Brick House is a two-story, I-house laid by the masons John L. Owen, Robert Owen, and John Powers for John S. Bratton, Sr. Construction of the house started in 1841 and was completed shortly after the death of John S. Bratton, Sr.'s death in 1843. This late example of Early Classical Revival, or Jeffersonian Classicism, served an atypical public mercantile function, in addition to having a private family use. The largest room of the first floor housed the Brattonsville Store. Prior to the

* Carroll, M.S. The Journal of M.S. Carroll (unpublished, 1924) 6-7; West, Jerry L. The Recon-struction Ku Klux Klan in York County South Carolina 1865-1877 (Jefferson, NC: McFarland & Company Inc. 2002) 123-125.

** United States Congress, Testimony Taken by the Joint Select Committee to Inquire into the Condition of Affairs in the late Insurrectionary States (Washington, DC: Government Printing Office, 1872) 709-710. https://archive.org/details/reportofjointsel04unit/page/710/mode/2up; Columbia Daily Phoenix (Columbia, SC: March 14, 1871) 2; Farris, Scott. Freedom on Trial: the Defeat and Demise of the Post Civil War Ku Klux Klan (Guilford, Connecticut: Lyons Press, 2020) 157. Martinez, Michael J. Carpetbaggers, Cavalry, and the Ku Klux Klan: Exposing the Invisible Empire During Reconstruction (Lanham, Maryland: Rowman and Littlefield Publishers Inc., 2007) 2; West, Jerry L. The Reconstruction Ku Klux Klan in York County South Carolina 1865-1877 (Jefferson, NC: McFarland & Company Inc. 2002) 71

Lemhouse / His Truth Is Marching On: Capt. James Williams and the Ku Klux Crisis in Reconstruction York County

American Civil War, the store also served as a post office and voting place. It is supposed that the coroner brought James Williams' body to the Brick House because the Brattonsville Store was the only quasi-civic location in the area.[*]

Fearing reprisal towards his family, John S. Bratton, Jr. Asked James Avery, reputed leader of the Ku Klux in York County, to send reinforcements. At least 15 to 20 men responded and kept watch with the Brattons, who had gathered together into one house for the night. in order to avert any further violence, Andy Tims, a lieutenant in Williams' militia company, turned over the company's weapons and the night passed without further incident.[**]

Violence towards African Americans across the South prompted the United States Congress to pass three pieces of legislation collectively known as the Enforcement Acts. The final act, known as the "Civil Rights Act of 1871", or the "Ku Klux Klan Act," passed only six weeks after Williams' lynching. President Grant signed the bill into law on April 20, 1871. President Grant used the power granted in the Civil Rights Act to suspend the writ of Habeas Corpus and impose martial law over a 9-county area in the South Carolina upstate, including York County.[***]

President Grant also sent four companies of the 7th US Cavalry to York County in mid-March of 1871 to reinforce five companies of the 18th US Infantry who had arrived in late February.

[*] Owen, John L. contract, May 6, 1843, Folder 33, Box 1, Bratton Family Paper Collection, South Caroliniana Library, University of South Carolina, Columbia; Mester, Joseph C., ed., "Homestead House Historic Structure Report" (Culture & Heritage Commission of York County, SC, 2021).

[**] United States Congress, *Testimony Taken by the Joint Select Committee to Inquire into the Condition of Affairs in the late Insurrectionary States* (Washington, DC: Government Printing Office, 1872) 709–710; *Columbia Daily Phoenix* (Columbia, SC: March 14, 1871) 2.

[***] West, Jerry L. The Reconstruction Ku Klux Klan in York County South Carolina 1865-1877 (Jefferson, NC: McFarland & Company Inc. 2002) 85; Pearl, Matthew, "K Troop: the Untold Story of the Eradication of the Original Ku Klux Klan," *Slate Online Magazine*, March 4, 2016. http://www.slate.com/articles/news_and_politics/history/2016/03/how_a_detachment_of_u_s_army_soldiers_smoked_out_the_original_ku_klux_klan.html

The cavalry commander, Lewis Merrill, conducted investigations into Ku Klux activity in the area. His notes became the basis for the Great South Carolina Ku Klux Trials, held in Columbia and Charleston in November of 1871 and April, 1872, respectively. Williams' murder trial was ultimately deferred to the Supreme Court of the United States making it the first trial born of the Enforcement Acts to make it to the Supreme Court.[*]

Ultimately, the Supreme Court declined to rule on Williams' case, deciding instead to send it back to a lower court. Of the 29 people initially indicted for their alleged involvement in Williams' lynching, only one, Robert Hayes Mitchell, stood trial. Eight others confessed. All nine were found guilty of the much lesser charge of conspiracy to violate Williams' civil rights and sentenced to 18 months imprisonment and a $100 fine. The remaining 20, including the alleged leaders, were never prosecuted in conjunction with Williams' murder.[**]

Both James Rufus Bratton and his older brother John Simpson Bratton, Jr. fled York County for their known association with the Ku Klux. James Rufus Bratton fled to London, Ontario seeking asylum. On June 10, 1872 Bratton was apprehended by federal authorities who sent him back to the United States to stand trial. The "kidnapping" of James Rufus Bratton excited widespread interest in Canada. The incident was brought to the House of Commons at Ottawa on June 11, 1872 and the Canadian Prime Minister, Sir John McDonald, opened a dialogue with the British ambassador at Washington. After two days in the

*"The Supreme Court and the KKK Act." *Yorkville Enquirer.* (York, SC: March 28, 1872); Zuczek, Richard. "The Federal Government's Attack on the Ku Klux Klan: a Reassessment," *South Carolina Historical Magazine,* Vol. 97, No. 1 (Jan. 1996); Pearl, Matthew, "K Troop: the Untold Story of the Eradication of the Original Ku Klux Klan," *Slate Online Magazine,* March 4, 2016. http://www.slate.com/articles/news_and_politics/history/2016/03/how_a_detachment_of_u_s_army_soldiers_smoked_out_the_original_ku_klux_klan.html

** Corbin, D.T. *South Carolina United States Circuit Court Vs. James Rufus Bratton et al.* December 9, 1871, Case # 168 (Atlanta, GA: National Archives)

York County jail, James Rufus Bratton posted bond and again fled to Ontario to escape prosecution for his alleged involvement in Williams' death. John S. Bratton, Jr. also fled York County and found exile in Memphis Tennessee.*

Reconstruction ended with the Compromise of 1877, an informal agreement among Congressmen to resolve the intensely disputed 1876 presidential election. Southern Democrats agreed to recognize the victory of Republican Rutherford B. Hayes in return for removal of federal troops from the South. As a result of the agreement, federal troops were withdrawn.

To many Republicans and Freedmen, the action was called "The Great Betrayal." Efforts to enforce civil rights laws were widely abandoned, leaving southern Blacks subject to growing racial inequities, oppression, and violence.**

By the time Hayes became president in 1877, the Grant administration had pardoned every convicted Ku Klux and prosecutions had ceased for violations of the Enforcement Acts. Even so, the Enforcement Acts and the subsequent trials led to the eventual disbandment of the first iteration of the Ku Klux. The Ku Klux would be reborn over forty years later following the romanticized depiction of the Ku Klux Klan in D.W. Griffith's film, *Birth of a Nation.****

In South Carolina, Democrats were poised to regain control of the state's government. Their efforts were led by gubernatorial hopeful Wade Hampton III, who promised to "redeem" South

* Landon, Fred. "The Kidnapping of Dr. Rufus Bratton," *Journal of Negro History* 10 (July 1925): 330-333; Landon, Fred. "Kidnapping on London Street in 1872 Developed Into International Incident," the London Free Press (London, Ontario: April 25, 1964); West, Jerry L. The Reconstruction Ku Klux Klan in York County South Carolina 1865-1877. McFarland & Company Inc. Jefferson, North Carolina. 2002.

** Foner, Eric. a *Short History of Reconstruction: 1863-1877* (New York: Harper Collins Publishers, 1990) 244-47.

*** West, Jerry L. The Reconstruction Ku Klux Klan in York County South Carolina 1865-1877 (Jefferson, NC: McFarland & Company Inc. 2002) 116.

Carolina from Reconstruction Era reforms. Aided by a vigilante group known as the "Red Shirts," Hampton coordinated a campaign of violence and intimidation to suppress black voters and win the governorship in 1876.*

In June 1878, South Carolina Governor Wade Hampton III brokered an agreement with President Hayes to have all charges against James Rufus Bratton dropped. He returned home to York County in November 1878. John S. Bratton, Jr., who fled to Memphis, Tennessee, returned to York County prior to his brother. On June 9, 1878, South Carolina Secretary of State, Robert M. Sims, conveyed Gov. Hampton's sentiments in a letter to John S. Bratton, Jr. stating, "...that all parties, like your brother...considered as Ku Klux, should come home...and rest assured on his word that they would not be disturbed...that he had every assurance of good faith in this matter from the President..."**

Though Capt. James Williams never received justice, his actions, and the actions of other brave African Americans, planted seeds of resistance that prompted decades of resistance in the 20th Century that eventually grew into the Civil Rights Movement of the 1950s and 1960s. Williams' legacy was best epitomized by South Carolina Attorney General Daniel H. Chamberlain during closing remarks at the South Carolina Ku Klux trials. Chamberlain marveled at Williams' "determination to protect the lives and liberties of his fellow-citizens..." and boldly declared that, "when the names of these conspirators, who murdered him, shall have rotted from the memory of men, some

* Foner, Eric. *a Short History of Reconstruction: 1863-1877* (New York: Harper Collins Publishers, 1990) 239-241

** "Return of Dr. Bratton," Yorkville Enquirer (York, SC: November 21, 1878); Wade Hampton to John S. Bratton, June 14, 1878, Bratton Paper Collection, South Caroliniana Library, University of South Carolina, Columbia, Box 2, Folder 252; R.M. Sims to John S. Bratton, June 9, 1878, Bratton Paper Collection, South Caroliniana Library, University of South Carolina, Columbia, Box 2, Folder 252; John S. Bratton to James R. Bratton, June 15, 1878, Bratton Paper Collection, South Caroliniana Library, University of South Carolina, Columbia, Box 2, Folder 252 generation will seek for marble white enough to bear the name of that brave negro captain."[*]

On January 4, 1872 (Emancipation Day) African Americans celebrated the contributions that Jim Williams made to the African American community by singing a song that was once reserved for the controversial abolitionist John Brown. After Brown's conviction and execution for the failed raid on the National Arsenal at Harpers Ferry, Virginia, his supporters memorialized his actions in lyrics meant to be sung to the tune of *Battle Hymn of the Republic*. The lyrics written for Williams are as follows:

Old Jim Williams's body lies a-mouldering in the grave,
While weeps the sons of bondage whom he ventured all to save;
But though he lost his life in struggling for the slave,
His truth is marching on.
Glory, Glory, Hallelujah!
His truth is marching on![**]

---

[*] Proceedings in the Ku Klux Trials at Columbia, S.C. in The United States Circuit Court, November Term, 1871 (New York, NY: Negro Universities Press, 1969) 394.

[**] "Emancipation Day." *the Chester Reporter.* Chester, South Carolina. January 4, 1872.

Everyday Life of Women in the New American Suburbs in the 1950s and 60s: Problem Statement and Research Model

Alexander Zhidchenko

Introduction

Presently, due to global trends in the world, the acceleration of sociocultural processes that impact different aspects of societies in various countries and regions is becoming more pronounced. Urbanization and the rapid advancement of information technology are among the factors contributing to this acceleration. These technologies progressively diminish both spatial and temporal distances. It is crucial to recognize that even in the 20th century, the world exhibited significant differences and had just embarked on the journey towards heightened globalization. One of the pivotal catalysts influencing this progression was the existence of two opposing systems — capitalist and communist — which competed during the Cold War.

The existence of these two conflicting socio-political and socio-economic systems shaped the developmental trajectories of numerous countries. This influence extended not only throughout the 20th century but also in the subsequent decades, touching diverse societal realms from governmental structures to the daily lives of common individuals. These shifts and disparities accumulated over each decade throughout the entirety of the Cold War era, undergoing transformation as a consequence of a global event. in this context, investigating how these modifications impacted the existences of regular people — millions of citizens from the USSR and the USA amidst the most intense standoff between these two global systems — assumes even greater significance.

The current study delves into the daily histories of these two nations during the 1950s and 1960s, focusing on emerging cities and urban zones. During this period, these newly established residential areas epitomized the evolving living standards pursued by the governments of both countries.

It's no coincidence that within Cold War historiography, one of the most noteworthy episodes during the verbal confrontation is unquestionably the Kitchen Debate. Its central focus was the standard of living, affluence, and consumption among citizens of both the United States and the USSR. These aspects garnered significant attention in the memoirs of both Nikita Khrushchev and Richard Nixon.

The Kitchen Debate comprises a series of spontaneous discussions (conducted through translators) between US Vice President Richard Nixon and Chairman of the Council of Ministers of the USSR Nikita Khrushchev. This dialogue took place on July 24, 1959, during the inauguration of the US National Exhibition showcasing American Industrial Products at the Sokolniki Park

Exhibition Center in Moscow. The exhibition featured a house which, according to the American organizers, was affordable for any American. The house was equipped with new appliances, showcasing the products available in the American consumer market. It was within the kitchen of this house that a particularly intense debate unfolded between the leaders of the two nations, encompassing discussions about the accomplishments and potentials of both communism and capitalism. This exchange was broadcasted on television in both countries, generating widespread attention.

Women's daily life, as recounted in oral memories, takes shape within this study as a narrative. Embedded within the context of the new cities of the 1950s and 1960s, it assumes the form of a text with three distinct interpretive angles. Firstly, it represents an objective reality that existed during this specific era in a particular location. Secondly, it embodies the subjective recollections of individuals engaged in the social process — the respondents — where every utterance holds a personal truth, if not always a historical one, from the standpoint of collective and individual memory. Thirdly, researchers themselves approach this narrative through the lens of their societal and scholarly backgrounds, incorporating memories within a defined historical context. in light of this, acknowledging the role of gender in both fieldwork and subsequent material analysis remains crucial (Warren, Hackney 2000).

The process of reconstructing the reality of "others", achieved through the analysis of one's own social experiences (even when separated by time, generations, territory, and more), as pursued in this study, is rooted in the theoretical foundation established by ethnographers and anthropologists widely acknowledged within the global academic community (Van Maanen 2011).

Historiography of women's urban everyday life in the USA

The historiography pertaining to the issue of daily life in American cities, alongside specific domains concerning the gender aspect of everyday life, forms a distinct segment of the research project's focus. Nonetheless, it's essential to highlight several noteworthy works relevant to our investigation. One endeavor that stands out is Kate Brown's book *Plutopia* (Brown 2015), which undertakes a comparative analysis of everyday life in American and Soviet cities during the mid-twentieth century. The gender perspective on urban everyday life is unveiled in Judy Giles' work *Salon and Suburbia: Domestic Identity, Social Strata, Feminism, and Modernity* (Giles 2004).

Regarding the reconstruction of women's everyday life within the context of social memory, this research topic falls within the purview of the gender perspective within historical scholarship. It's noteworthy to acknowledge the contributions of N.L. Pushkareva (2019) in addressing issues related to women's social memory and their everyday life (Veremenko, Lyubichankovsky 2019). Drawing upon the theoretical and methodological foundations laid out in these works, it can be inferred that the planned study will unfold at the crossroads of everyday history, emerging local history, museology, and will also be guided by an ethno-gender approach (Laslett, Brenner 1989; Hirdman 1991; Pateman 1998).

From a thematic and chronological perspective, the historiography of women's everyday urban life in the USA during the mid-twentieth century can be delineated into three primary stages. The initial stage, spanning from the late 1960s to the late 1980s, is marked by the swift urbanization within American society and researcher' endeavors to elucidate the dynamic social phenomena that emerge amidst this backdrop, encompassing ethnic minorities, gender dynamics, and socially marginalized sectors. This phase can be tentatively termed the "gender-urban" stage.

Sylvia F. Fava, an urbanist and sociologist, significantly contributed to the advancement of issues linked to women's lives in American suburbs. Her work delved into the phase of suburbanization that unfolded on the fringes of metropolitan regions after World War II (Fava 1985). This era witnessed the United States transforming into a nation where suburbs constituted the predominant residential domain, accommodating the majority of the American population. Many of these suburban areas originated organically from existing suburbs rather than being decentralized from inner cities. Consequently, the succeeding generation of Americans, born and raised in these suburbs, have transitioned from one suburban area to another over their lifetimes, lacking direct exposure to city living with high population density and the challenges prevalent in the central zones of metropolitan regions (Fava 1979).

Works of a historical and sociological nature that exhibit a relatively subdued focus on the gender aspect include Zane Miller's study *Suburb: neighborhood and community in Forest Park, Ohio, 1935-1976* (Miller 1981). The research delves into the history of Forest Park as a segment of the broader community narrative within suburban (and urban) America. Within this, the author uncovers the perspective prevalent in the 1950s and 1960s, wherein the notion held that suburbs truly developed post-World War II. This viewpoint gave rise to explanations concerning the implications and outcomes of suburban growth, often juxtaposing the suburban community against the concept of the "city". Nevertheless, it was the widespread migration of Americans to the suburbs that facilitated the emergence of a fresh generation within civil society. This generation took charge of their daily concerns, paving the way for the establishment of local public organizations that enabled various social groups, including women, ethnic communities, and professional associations, to fulfill their potential (Ibid.: 18-19).

In 1986, historian Cynthia Sturgis authored an article discussing the establishment of a supportive environment for women's daily lives — a concept known as the urban model — within rural settings, using Utah as a case study. The issue at hand was that in the first half of the 20th century, the combination of relative isolation and demanding agricultural labor prompted women to forsake their rural origins and migrate to cities. However, during this period, the government of Utah endeavored to create an "urban environment" model, aimed at reshaping the lives of rural women. This model involved elevating the status of the housewife to that of a recognized profession, enhancing the aesthetics of the agricultural surroundings, introducing contemporary conveniences, and shifting the prevailing economic role of the rural housewife from a producer to a consumer of goods. In the initial decades of the 20th century, agricultural publications and the Utah Agricultural College advocated for the principles of modernization, and the implementation of rural electrification revolutionized women's work on farms. This study holds significance for the topic at hand, as this model elucidates the preconditions that shaped the urban everyday lives of women in the mid-20th century, particularly within small towns and suburbs (Sturgis 1986).

During the 1980s, economist Anna Markusen embarked on a series of publications that delved into the realm of women's roles within American suburbs during the Cold War era (Markusen 1978; Markusen 1989). Her exploration illuminated the influence of gender, particularly the power dynamics inherent in a patriarchal society, on the formation and arrangement of urban and suburban spaces, ultimately shaping gender relations. Markusen stresses that this patriarchal structure has a "deeply formed

American urban spatial structure" and "promotes single-family suburban housing."

Markusen advocated against the inequitable division of labor between working men and women shouldering domestic responsibilities. Notably, women within families handled grocery shopping and meal preparation, while professionals in the food industry performed the same tasks for remuneration. These dynamics, as the author contended, were unjust due to the disproportional impact on women, who were primarily responsible for household and childcare duties, often while maintaining external employment. This spatial segregation between urban and suburban areas corresponded with the gender-based division of labor. Consequently, it transpired that household contributions weren't equitable: women usually performed more domestic and child-rearing work than men. Consequently, only men reaped the benefits of marriage agreements and the migration of the traditional American family to the suburbs (Markusen 1980).

Indeed, the construction of suburban housing developments during the 1950s and 1960s contributed to the privatization of family life and the reinforcement of firmly divided gender roles. Suburbs were situated increasingly distant from central cities, where most paid employment was located. This resulted in lengthier commutes for men, reducing their available time for family interactions. This, in turn, intensified the isolation felt by women, particularly considering the common presence of only one family car primarily used by commuting men. Moreover, the concept of privacy within the family home translated to increased domestic responsibilities for women, as suburban housing layouts often failed to facilitate communal domestic work. in reality, architectural designs, often influenced by Art Nouveau aesthetics, inadvertently amplified the domestic workload for women. With large windows, open floor plans, fireplaces, and elaborate kitchens, a heightened emphasis on cleanliness and tidiness prevailed. in essence, the design of suburban communities and homes perpetuated the notion that a woman's functions were limited to "housework" and parenting (Markusen 1981).

However, opposition to the idea of women facing constraints due to suburban living in the post-war decades emerged. in 1979, an article by Marilyn Rubin titled *Debunking the myth: working women in suburbia* challenged the perception of women being confined to housewife roles. Amidst criticism of the "enslavement of women as housewives" during the late 1970s and early 1980s, Rubin briefly traced the evolution of American suburbs since the 1920s, portraying a typical suburban family consisting of a working husband and a stay-at-home housewife-mother. She dispelled the notion of non-working suburban women, using 1950s workforce statistics as evidence (Rubin 1979).

Additionally, Nancy Walker tackled the theme of humor and gender roles within American suburbs post-World War II. Prominent female writers of the late 1940s and 1950s employed humor to depict women's roles within families and their interactions with husbands, children, pets, and neighbors. Writers such as Shirley Jackson, Betty Macdonald, Phyllis McGinley, Margaret Halsey, and Jean Kerr used humor to veil their hostility towards domestic life.

The second stage, spanning from the late 1980s to the early 2000s, witnesses an increased emphasis on studying the role of women within families and their social significance within the new American suburbs in the postwar decades. Unlike the preceding stage, these works shift focus away from closely connecting social issues to the broader historical context of the American political system and rapid urbanization. Instead, they center attention on women as a steadfast support system for strong American families, standing shoulder-to-shoulder with their husbands. This phase can be aptly labeled as the "family-oriented" stage. in this context, a pivotal article by Kim England, titled *Changing Suburbs, Changing Women: Geographic Perspectives on Suburban Women and Suburbanization*, published in 1993 in the journal *Frontiers: a Journal of Women Studies*, holds significance for our inquiry (England 1993).

Kim England's work resides within the realm of "feminist geography", an exploration of the interplay between gender and urban spatial structures. Recognizing that gender-based aspects play a pivotal role in the distribution of resources, objects, and opportunities, England, aligned with the proponents of this theory, emphasizes its significance in structuring urban spaces. Residential locations, workplaces, transportation networks, and overall city layouts reflect the expectations of a patriarchal capitalist society regarding activities, their locations, timing, and the individuals responsible. in turn, the city reinforces and perpetuates gender-based beliefs that underpin it. England asserts that gender identity takes shape within and through space, with its particular form imprinted within specific spatial configurations. Consequently, the gender-based cultural norm deeply shapes and influences the very nature and structure of the city. Through a meticulous examination of the urban landscape, valuable insights can be gleaned regarding the cultural processes it embodies and upholds. in her article, England applies these ideas within the context of the evolving suburban life and daily experiences of suburban women in the United States during the mid- to latter-half of the 20th century (England 1993: 24-25).

The structure of the article begins by scrutinizing the geographical literature regarding post-World War II suburban settlements and the lives of women within them. It then delves into how specific societal shifts have influenced the experiences of suburban women, with employment opportunities being particularly noteworthy. Nevertheless, the spatial layout of numerous suburbs inadequately supported women attempting to balance multiple roles, and researchers highlighted the spatial constraints women encountered across different states. The subsequent segment of the article examines the stages in the evolution of women's social roles within the suburbs. Feminist scholars underscore that post-war suburban housing and neighborhoods were planned and developed by governmental bodies, developers, planners, and architects adhering to patriarchal and heterosexual presumptions about "suitable" gender roles and sub-roles. Thus, post-war residential suburbanization was structured around the notion of dichotomous spheres: the "private" sphere encompassing consumption, reproduction, home, family, and household was deemed women's domain, while the "public" sphere involving production, wage labor, and political engagement was associated with men. The concept of these dual spheres was further bolstered by the emergence of professional "experts", particularly doctors and psychologists, who emphasized the necessity for "restructuring" families. Accordingly, nurturing the mother-child relationship was portrayed as paramount for the healthy development of the post-war generation. Childcare was tailored in accordance with Freudian theories of child development, advising mothers (and still advocating) to attend to children's social, mental, and physical growth, as well as their well-being, discipline, and cleanliness. Simultaneously, the author underscores that post-war family-centric suburbs were marketed as an ideal environment for raising (white) children in heterosexual, middle-class, single-family households. These suburbs offered white women a novel family model grounded in heightened consumption of mass-produced goods and services, distancing them from the challenges and harsh realities of manufacturing, criminality, and destructive urban environments (England 1993: 25-28).

In the broader realm of American women's history, particularly concerning the daily lives of American women, a significant contribution is made by the review *When Women Get Together: Black Women, Working Women, and History* by Molly Mitchell (Mitchell 1937). Although Mitchell's focus centers on women whose rights were infringed or discriminated against, her review showcases extensive analytical work addressing issues interwoven with the daily lives of urban women throughout the 20th century, rooted in earlier historical periods.

A distinctive subsection within the historiography of women's urban daily life is associated with the Women's History Department of the American Historical Association.

Historian and sociologist Camilla Stivers provides insights into aspects of 20th-century U.S. social development through the lens of a gender-focused approach to urban studies in her interdisciplinary work *Bureau Men, Settlement Women: Constructing Public Administration in the Progressive Era* (Strivers 2000). From Stivers' perspective, gender shapes public life during the 20th century in a manner akin to its impact on private life. During the period of governmental system evolution, the connection between masculinity and public authority becomes conspicuous. The early 20th century witnessed Americans adhering to the distinct social roles delineated between women and men during the 19th century. These gendered assumptions resonated as prominently in social contexts as they did in households and daily life. With respect to the development of municipal authorities in the 20th century, Stivers affirms the hypothesis that "gender relations are the primary aspect of social organization," mostly rooted in cultural determinants rather than biological factors, and not merely resultant from individual personality development. in essence, Stivers asserts that gender is not just a superficial facade but rather a definitive component of social existence that significantly influences municipal governance and everyday life (Ibid.: 10-11).

Susan Seagart's exploration into the ethno-gender dimensions of urbanization in American cities, particularly New York's Harlem district, concluded that extensive suburban housing tracts marked the culmination of a growing spatial and functional division between the private sector population and industrial districts and business centers. This segregation led to the emergence of what Seagart terms "male cities" and "female suburbs," as the public sphere of the city became associated with masculinity, gradually pushing women out of the workforce and into their prescribed place within the home (Saegart 1981).

The everyday lives of women in American suburbs have also been uncovered through various scholarly articles devoted to individual episodes of domestic life. For instance, Alison Clark delved into the influence of Tupper products on American society. Introduced by Earl Tupper in 1938, Tupperware comprised molded polyethylene containers. The innovation behind Tupperware lay in its marketing strategy, which perfectly aligned with post-war developments in the United States where women predominantly assumed roles as homemakers and consumers. Tupperware parties seamlessly integrated into this societal framework, becoming a ubiquitous household necessity that women not only purchased but also endorsed through hosting or attending themed gatherings. This marketing approach provided informal employment opportunities for housewives, ultimately making Tupperware an emblem of modernity, mass marketing, and a staple in American daily life (Clarke 1994).

The third stage characterizes the present state of historiography on this subject, encompassing the period from the early 2000s to the current day. While intrinsically linked to the overarching historical context that shaped women's everyday lives across various historical epochs, this stage focuses on personal stories and biographies, transforming depersonalized narratives into the experiences and memories of specific individuals. During the 1950s and 1960s, thousands of American women resided in suburbs nationwide, and modern historians have now directed their research towards these individuals. On one hand, the temporal distance allowed for more objective conclusions, with less emphasis on specific political or socio-economic nuances. On the other hand, the imminent passing of the previous generation of that era prompted historians to gather first-hand accounts from young people who lived in the initial post-war decades. Employing methods such as oral history and other post-non-classical research approaches, the boundaries of understanding women's daily lives have expanded significantly, presenting it in a fresh language and enriched with new facts and figures, highlighting the lives of ordinary American women, be they homemakers or business owners. This stage of historiography can be aptly termed "personally oriented."

Within this third historiographic stage ("person-oriented"), Judy Giles' book *the Parlour and the Suburb: Domestic Identities, Class, Femininity and Modernity* (Giles 2004) serves as a pivotal work offering comprehensive insights into women's urban everyday lives during the 20th century. Giles spotlights a critical dilemma faced by suburban women in the post-war decades: to wholly dedicate themselves to homemaking and child-rearing or to pursue careers and receive professional and personal recognition. For many women, the former path was deemed the most secure and even evolved into an ideal and aspiration entrenched within mass consciousness and popular culture.

Giles identifies the city as the locus of modernity, accessible through sociology, historiography, geography, or literary criticism. However, the portrayal of the city as a "public stage" for the performances of contemporary life reinforces a rigid division between public and private spheres. Giles dedicates her book to exploring how modernity was expressed and envisioned within the private world of women, as well as the public discourse surrounding this private existence.

Victoria Hesford's work (Hesford 2005) unveils the issues surrounding the everyday lives of women in American families within the context of the Cold War.

In the 1980s, Nancy Walker delved into humor and gender roles, a topic revisited from a different perspective in 2011 by Charlotte Haygood. Haygood's work, *Rethinking the Nuclear Family: Judith Merril's Shadow on the Hearth and Domestic Science Fiction* (Hagood 2011), delves into the complex portrayal of the "enslaved" woman within the household of American suburbs through the lens of literary representation.

The author's focus is on Judith Merrill's 1950 science fiction novel *Shadow on the Hearth* and Betty Friedan's 1963 classic *the Feminine Mystique*. These works center on an American suburban home, one of the many that emerged in the United States after World War II, serving as a microcosm of a nationwide social crisis. The new norm of women's everyday lives, as validated through numerous interviews and articles from the period, formed the basis of Friedan's research and was a direct outcome of radical shifts in middle-class life patterns, including the rise of households that kept many women "in their power." the ideology that "crafted housewife mothers who never had a chance to be anything else," becoming a "model for all women," was grounded in the "concrete, ultimate, internal aspects of female existence" of past generations, but at the same time permeated every facet of modern family life, "from women's sexual desires to the boxed cakes they prepared for their families" (Ibid.: 1006-1007). Termed a classic statement of second-wave feminism, these novels also held a close political connection to the broader historical context. The looming threat of nuclear war during the Cold War era created a sense of urgency, potentially rallying

American families within suburban communities. Yet, as women fought for their families' safety and global stability, the concept of a "private paradise" in the suburban havens, where women solely trusted men to shield their families, came into question (Ibid.: 1028-1029).

A distinct historiographic segment within the exploration of women's urban everyday life in the mid-twentieth century is dedicated to the complexities of Levittowns. Levittown is the collective term for seven significant suburban housing developments established in the United States by William Levitt and his company, Levitt & Sons. Constructed post-World War II for returning veterans and their families, these communities presented appealing alternatives to cramped city dwellings. in the late 1940s, an agreement between the US Veterans Committee and the Federal Housing Administration allowed veterans to purchase housing in these new suburban hubs with substantial subsidies.

However, contradictions emerged during the creation of Levittowns, touching on issues such as racial discrimination (Wolfinger 2012), labor and trade unionism (Anderson 2005), and the transformation of women's social roles. The latter subject is particularly explored by Rosalynn Bexendall and Elizabeth Ewen, who documented the daily lives of post-World War II suburban women through in-person interviews with women residing in three Nassau County suburbs: Levittown (designated as a mass housing suburb for white single-family homes), Freeport (selected for its racially diverse established community), and Roosevelt, representing an almost entirely black suburb (Baxandall, Ewen 1990). Published in 1990 in the Long Island Historical Journal under the title *Painting the Windows: the Changing Role of Women in Suburbia, 1945-2000*, this work not only delves into the history of women in post-war suburbs but also compares real-life experiences to prevailing societal ideals.

Concluding, the authors note that the post-war "move to the suburbs" physically distanced many American families from their relatives while forming new social bonds in their new residential locales. in the three types of suburbs examined, the authors highlight the unity inherent in these communities, particularly beneficial for women who could rely on neighbors, friends, and emerging community networks for support, child safety, and more (Ibid.: 106-107).

The geographical scope of studying women's urban everyday life in mid-twentieth-century United States is quite extensive. The research draws from materials across multiple American states, yielding publications that directly or indirectly touch upon this subject. a closer examination of some of these works is warranted.

It's important to highlight that this pattern of research began to emerge as early as the 1990s (during the second stage, which we have provisionally identified). However, a more comprehensive exploration of regional history and the extraction of broader insights from local sources largely gained traction in the 2000s. For instance, Linda Hartranft's dissertation, *the Ninth Decade: Six Central Ohio Women*, delved into the daily lives of Ohio women in the 20th century through the use of oral history (Hartranft 1992). Drawing from family biographies, each centered around one of the six chosen elderly women, the study addresses a wide array of topics connected to everyday life, migration, social anthropology, and more.

Another work from Ohio State that holds relevance to our subject is Jeffrey Hammond's *Ohio States: a Twentieth-Century Midwestern* (Hammond 2002). This book draws from an extensive array of personal sources, including memoirs and materials from the author's family history. The gender aspect is prominently evident within the context of daily life analysis, which encompasses typical male, female, and children's experiences, as well as family pastimes overall, particularly during the 1950s and 60s.

Main stages of the research project

Research into the everyday lives of women in the new cities and urban areas of the USSR during the 1950s and 60s became an integral part of a comprehensive research project. The findings from this study, along with subsequent work, were compiled and published in the educational and scholarly manual titled *History of My City: the Historical and Cultural Space of New Cities and Urban Areas of Russia in the Mid-20th Century* (Zhidchenko 2016).

In the current phase, the intention is to extend the investigation to encompass the daily lives of women in new cities and suburbs that emerged in the United States during the mid-20th century. This section, therefore, forms a crucial component of a broad comparative study examining the lives of women in new cities and urban areas of both the USSR and the USA during the 1950s and 60s.

The proposed research model stands on interdisciplinary foundations and draws from methodologies in the history of everyday life, new local history, oral history, cultural and civilizational landscape theory (CCL), as well as the gender approach. Moreover, a significant portion of the work involves historical comparative analysis, facilitating a juxtaposition of women's daily experiences in two distinct types of urban settings during the 1950s and 60s – the "American" and the "Soviet."

This approach amalgamates conventional methods that chronicle the history of a local entity with interdisciplinary methodologies focused on everyday life's history and contemporary theories aimed at dissecting complex phenomena like cities and urban cultures. This amalgamation gives rise to a theoretical framework. Initially conceptualized for the reconstruction of the history of a unique "Soviet urban area," this framework was initially applied to multiple new cities of the USSR from the 1950s and 60s. a similar model entails piecing together the history of a localized entity within the larger historical context of the nation, leveraging various facets to provide a comprehensive depiction. Subsequently, within each facet, similar reconstruction can occur, encompassing factors such as regional history, a holistic view of the population's daily lives, and more.

For the first time, this model will be tested on materials extracted from the urban landscape of a non-socialist nation. The underlying concept of this scientific reconstruction of the history of everyday life in new urban areas of the 1950s and 60s involves the development of an experimental research model composed of several components. Primarily, an exploration of the architectural and planning landscape – the foundation of the new district – will form the material environment of the urban cultural space. Additionally, the study will hinge on the analysis of social infrastructure and its evolution, tracking shifts in everyday practices connected to the confined territory of the new urban area. Finally, the aim is to spotlight the cultural attributes that emerged among the population within this space through the lens of everyday life history. Consequently, a comprehensive narrative of the history of everyday life in new urban areas will materialize, capable of being applied to diverse metropolitan areas not only within the USSR and the former socialist bloc but also within capitalist nations such as the United States of America.

The first phase of the research project

As previously discussed, the initial phase of this research project delved into the everyday life of the new cities built in the USSR during the 1950s and 60s. This investigation encompassed cities and urban areas with diverse profiles:

Working cities and urban areas with various industrial focuses, including those associated with the oil industry. This category consisted of cities such as Omsk Town of Oil Workers, Angarsk, Salavat, and Octyabrsky, which were linked to oil production, as well as Volzhsky, a hydroengineering city. The selection of these specific industries was deliberate, as they emerged as critical components of the USSR's post-war industrialization.

Science cities, including the Novosibirsk Akademgorodok and satellite cities of Moscow – Dubna and Zelenograd. These scientific centers were established during the Cold War era, with a special emphasis on nuclear physics research.

The second phase of the research project

Transitioning into the second phase of the research project, the focus shifts to the study of urban everyday life in new cities that experienced significant development during the 1950s. This period was marked by robust economic growth in the US and the establishment of societal values and norms that profoundly impacted the 20th century.

The research will encompass several cities across diverse geographical regions of the United States, with their primary development occurring in the 1950s. Some of these cities include Henderson (Nevada), Arvada (Colorado), Garden City (Idaho), and Artesia (California). The findings are intended to be presented in a textbook designed for students and schoolchildren from both Russia and foreign nations. Additionally, an educational exhibition project dedicated to everyday life in the new cities of the USA and the USSR during the mid-20th century is envisaged.

Arvada (Colorado), Garden City (Idaho), Artesia (California), etc. The results are planned to be published in the textbook for students and schoolchildren of Russia and foreign countries, as well as the creation of an educational exhibition project dedicated

Zhidchenko / Everyday Life of Women in the New American Suburbs in the 1950s and 60s: Problem Statement and Research Model

173

to everyday life in the new cities of the USA and the USSR in the mid-20th century.

The future city of **Henderson** was founded in the early 1940s during World War II in connection with the construction of the Base Magnesium Plant. Henderson quickly became the main supplier of magnesium in the United States, which was called the "wonder metal" of World War II. in 1947, magnesium production was no longer necessary for defense, and most of BMP's 14,000 employees left. However, Nevada authorities decided to save the city and supported other industries and small businesses. Henderson was registered in the spring of 1953 as a city with a population of 7,410 by the forces of representatives of local industry, and quickly began to grow in the 1950s and 60s.

Arvada is a city in the State of Colorado that appeared in the 19th century as a result of the discovery of gold deposits here. However, it is interesting to us in the history of Arvada that the main growth of this city occurred precisely in the 1950-60s. So, historians notes that Arvada grew rapidly during the latter half of the 20th century as a suburb of nearby Denver, the state capital. Arvada became a Statutory City on October 31, 1951, and a Home Rule Municipality on July 23, 1963.

The village of **Artesia** was established upon the completion of the Artesia School District on May 3, 1875. It was named for the many flowing artesian wells in the area, which made the village ideal for farming and agriculture. in the 1920s and 1930s, Dutch and Portuguese farmers developed Artesia into one of the most important dairy districts in Southern California. After World War II, as with many other cities in the region, Artesia was pressured by developers to build residential tracts. The city of Dairy Valley was incorporated in 1956, and later became the city of Cerritos.

The main development of **Garden City** in Idaho also occurred in the 1950s. The village, founded in the 19th century, got its name because local farmers recruited Chinese migrants to work, who built green gardens here. After 1949, Garden City began to actively develop as a suburb of Boise. After the ban on creating gambling establishments in Boise, it was in Garden City that many entertainment centers, as well as restaurants and hotels began to open. in the same period, new residential quarters were actively built here.

Also, the city of **Lawrence** in the state of Kansas fell into the scope of research on women's everyday life in the mid-twentieth century. Although this city is not new for the 1950s and 60s. and was founded in the eighteenth century, it is of interest to us as a university center, where many women who come from other cities and states of the United States live. Their memoirs restore the general historical context of women's everyday life and complement it.

While these cities were initially chosen for investigation, ongoing research and in-depth exploration during the study may lead to adjustments to the list. This could include the inclusion of cities like Levittowns, which were established as social experiments in the postwar era, and industrial cities that emerged around metallurgical, coal, oil, or engineering industries during the middle of the 20th century. Such industrial cities often came into being during or after World War II, contributing to what is now known as the "Rust Belt" in the US.

This list of cities was selected at the preparatory stage of the study. However, after the start of research in the United States, with a deeper immersion in this topic, this list has been adjusted. in particular, it is impossible not to touch upon such cities as Levittowns, which were built in the postwar decade as a social experiment. Of course, a large number of works of a historical and sociological nature have been published at present, concerning such a type of cities as Levittown[*]. However, the use of the proposed research model related to everyday life in the new urban space has not yet been applied on the materials of these cities.

They are also industrial cities that sprang up around the metal, coal, oil or engineering industries in the middle of the 20th century. The cities that arose during the Second World War or the first post-war decades around new large enterprises, including those that are now part of the so-called "US rust belt" (Rust Belt).

Sources for the reconstruction of women's urban everyday life in the United States in the 1950s and 60s

Among the sources to be utilized for this study, the following crucial groups should be distinguished:

Legislative Acts: These are the primary documents that delineated the overarching trajectories of US social and economic development during the 1950s and 60s.

Office Documentation: This constitutes a quintessential source for exploring everyday life history. It encompasses a variety of current documents, including references, reports, regulations, project documentation, and more.

Periodicals: This substantial category of historical sources provides insights into the daily routines of the new American cities and suburbs of the 1950s and 60s. The author conducted a comprehensive review of key US federal periodicals from this period to extract pertinent information. Additionally, an exhaustive examination of selected local periodicals from cities chosen as study subjects was conducted, including Henderson (Nevada), Arvada (Colorado), Garden City (Idaho), and Artesia (California).

---

* Ferrer Margaret Lundrigan, Navarra Tova. Levittown. The First 50 Years. Arcadia Publishing. 1997; Kushner David. Levittown. Two Families, One Tycoon, and the Fight for Civil Rights in America's Legendary Suburb. Bloomsbury Publishing. 2022.

Sources of Personal Origin: This group of sources stands out as one of the most significant in this endeavor. It can be subdivided into three distinct blocks. Firstly, it encompasses recorded memories of individuals who lived in the new suburbs and cities of the United States during the 1950s and 60s. These individuals ranged from children of that era to the burgeoning adult population, establishing families and raising children. This segment of historical sources closely intertwines with the methodology of "oral history."

Although the source collection was conducted in Lawrence (Kansas), most women were born and raised in the suburbs of other major and medium-sized US cities that came into existence in the mid-20th century.

The recollections covered facets such as the lives of the respondents' mothers, daily life routines, interior house settings, interactions with relatives and friends, and participation in suburban public life. a distinct section of inquiries pertained to the Cold War, including women's perspectives on the USSR and anti-communist propaganda.

The second block pertains to other sources of personal origin, encompassing materials related to family biographies, family photo albums, inherited household items, documents from family archives, and more.

The third block encompasses published memoirs not only from ordinary American women but also from renowned figures who lived and played significant roles in shaping American history during the 1950s and 60s. These include the memoirs of distinguished politicians, public figures, cultural and artistic luminaries, whose recollections provide a subjective perspective on American history and everyday life. It is crucial to acknowledge that this "subjective viewpoint" of objective reality is of immense importance to us, as it represents the reflections and evaluations of witnesses and participants in the events under study.

Specialized Sources: This category encompasses a complex array of literature from non-historical fields of knowledge that directly or indirectly relate to the subject of this study. Primarily from the 1950s and 60s, these publications encompass textbooks, manuals, reference materials, monographs, and specialized publications on architecture, urban planning, housing and utilities, commerce, entertainment industry creation, home economics, domestic life, and more.

Cartographic materials represent a non-standard type of source within classical historical science.

Cinema and photo documents constitute a comprehensive collection of historical resources covering various visual sources. Each of these sources should be examined from specific perspectives and methodologies. Firstly, this category includes documentary photographs and video materials captured during the 1950s and 60s. They were created for diverse target audiences and with varying objectives, such as showcasing the success of new housing construction in American suburbs, illustrating changing living standards as a result of successful social policies, and motivating people to take action.

Secondly, mass media production during the studied period, intended to convey information, entertainment, and engagement, played a pivotal role in the everyday lives of American society in the 1950s and 60s. This source's significance lies in the growing influence of television and visual media on the daily routines of US citizens. a considerable portion of daily life was intertwined with the consumption of these resources.

Thirdly, a notable aspect in traditional historical studies, gaining recent relevance, is feature films depicting the everyday life of the American middle class in the suburbs of the 1950s and 60s. However, considering cinema as a source requires a critical lens, evaluating the subjectivity inherent in the approach of directors, authors, and producers through cross-analysis with other sources.

Conducting field surveys of the studied locations at the present stage aims to identify the cultural and historical dynamics of the urban landscape. These surveys follow the methodology proposed by Omsk city culture historians. a comprehensive examination facilitates the identification of architectural and planning features of urban areas, as well as the determination of coordinates within the local urban cultural space.

Museum collections represent another crucial type of source. They prove invaluable for solving a wide array of research inquiries linked to the representation of social memory during the 1950s and 60s. These collections also contribute to the reconstruction of everyday life in the American suburbs of this era. Given the significant attention historical museums dedicate to this period in their exhibitions, modern museum technologies effectively bring the reality of this bygone era to life. Visitors are drawn to their curated collections, information displays, oral narratives, and memoirs. The close collaboration between historical and local history museums and the local historical community greatly benefits researchers. This collaboration substantially enhances not only the exhibition series but also the overall semantic content of each subject within a specific historical era.

Components of the research model of women's urban everyday life in the USA in the 1950s and 60s

Drawing from an extensive source base and a synthesis of historiographic material, the study encompasses a range of issues, which can be outlined as follows:

Firstly, the concept of women's everyday life emerges as a compilation of behavioral traits within an individual and society. This phenomenon is intricately linked to the urban socio-cultural environment. When considering the American suburbs of the 1950s and 60s, the prime residence of the middle-class Americans, a thorough analysis of the standard suburban setting is essential. This analysis involves dissecting the life space, with individual residential structures being the primary structural units housing American families.

Additionally, the intentions and visions of American planners, urbanists, and developers in shaping this new urban landscape warrant examination. Given the backdrop of the Cold War, during this period, a competition between capitalist and communist systems was underway. Thus, the architects of "model" suburban communities had to design these territories to ensure optimal comfort for the residents.

In line with this, the subsequent issue that emerges is the interplay between the "ideal" and "real" dimensions of daily life. The authorities of the United States aimed to elevate living standards and nurture a healthy, well-fed generation whose fundamental needs were met. Official video chronicles, feature films, documentaries, advertisements, magazines, and other visual products of the 1950s and 60s propagate notions of happiness and contented living among American families. These portray standards of behavior and daily routines, such as families convening in well-appointed living rooms of spacious, well-lit houses where parents engage with newspapers or books while children play or interact with pets. Kitchens are equipped with refrigerators and a range of household appliances aimed at easing women's domestic chores. Garages house cars that facilitate family trips to other states or visits to relatives in neighboring cities. Friendly neighbors foster a close-knit community where everyone knows each other and social interactions flourish.

This "ideal" facet of daily life is extensively reflected across various sources from the 1950s and 60s, including films, newspapers, magazines, and video chronicles. On the flip side, an array of sources can unveil the reality of daily life with its socio-economic challenges, ethnic dynamics, criminal and social disruptions, and the inherent contradictions within the everyday existence of the new American cities and suburbs of the mid-20th century. Testimonies from elderly residents who lived in American suburbs during this period provide insight, although these accounts often idealize the past. Archival documents and periodicals, unlike their counterparts in the USSR, lack comprehensive ideological contexts.

Thirdly, the predicament of shaping American suburbs is intertwined with the intricate web of internal contradictions within post-war American society. Ethnic minorities often encountered restrictions on settling in new suburbs. The drive to create an "ideal" domestic environment led certain strata of the complex social structure to be excluded, exacerbating societal contradictions. Yet, instances emerged where entirely African-American "neighborhoods" were established. Despite these communities having slightly lower living standards compared to white suburban counterparts, they exemplified the realization of the "American dream" for a significant segment of the population.

Minnesota Historical Center's exposition spotlights an example of an ideal suburban community comprising African American families in Minneapolis. Personal narratives, photographs, video chronicles, and personal artifacts vividly depict this model of everyday life during those years. The intricate matter of ethnic tensions within American suburbs of the 1950s and 60s necessitates dedicated historical inquiry, albeit with occasional mentions in our study.

The fourth set of objectives revolves around the formation of an ideal American home. While certain American families in the 1950s and 60s either bought or inherited pre-World War II houses that remained comfortable and habitable, the massive suburban migration during these decades prompted millions of families to construct or purchase new houses, with updated layouts.

During this period, American architects devised a series of comfortable suburban homes catering to families. The interior and exterior design aimed to meet ideal living standards while adapting to changing trends, work and leisure practices, and a new lifestyle for Americans.

The fifth aspect delves into gender-specific concerns. a pivotal issue pertains to the "enslavement of women," who in postwar American families often adopted the role of homemakers. This situation represents both a significant social achievement within the American economic and political systems and a situation that imposed material, physical, psychological, and personal constraints on women, complicating their self-realization. This study aims to discern whether this issue objectively mirrors social reality or whether it is a journalistic or scientifically propagated construct influenced by feminist-oriented theories.

The project necessitates the construction of "gender spaces", the spaces of feminine and masculine urban everyday life in the USA during the 1950s and 60s. This research model, previously tested on mid-20th century Soviet new cities, is being adapted for American contexts.

The sixth set of issues spans a spectrum of women's social memory concerns. The new American suburbs and cities developed during the 1950s and 60s created distinct urban spaces, characterized by the spirit, style, preferences, needs, and mentalities of that era. However, the original inhabitants are now departing, leaving behind "neighborhoods" for a new generation – their grandchildren and great-grandchildren. These descendants either purchase these houses or make them their own. As these "neighborhoods" change to suit the preferences and needs of new occupants, a new realm of everyday life is forged within the framework of the old city that prevailed during their ancestors' time.

Importantly, unlike houses constructed before the 1950s and 60s, these residential buildings are often not designated as historical or cultural heritage sites in the USA. State, local, and private initiatives seldom undertake the task of preserving their architectural and external integrity, nor do they strive to retain their "family biography" and "family memory." Yet, numerous questions arise. Why do contemporary American families prefer houses built in those mid-20th-century years over modern alternatives? This issue is tied to the growing trend of retro-style, including mid-century modern aesthetics from the 1950s and 60s. Furniture and appliance manufacturers, advertising, and other sectors exploit this style. The phenomenon generates a unique response, particularly among younger generations who didn't live through that era. Nostalgia for the past merges with an engagement in history, connecting individuals to a broader narrative encompassing various events of the mid-20th century.

Conclusion

The research model presented in the paper involves a comprehensive analysis of a wide array of historical sources, with the objective of reconstructing the daily life of women in new American cities constructed during the 1950s and 60s. Drawing upon the scrutinized historiography and the outlined problem landscape, the main steps of the study and pertinent social processes have been formulated. Among the pivotal issues are women's existence within the context of burgeoning consumer society and the economic upswing in the United States during the 1950s and 60s. Furthermore, it delves into the American population's migration to suburban areas following World War II, the interplay of gender roles within American families, and the potential for women's self-realization.

The chosen cities serve as novel local focal points that have hitherto remained beyond the scope of historians' interest (unlike the more widely recognized and studied Levittown or Garden City).

These selected instances represent the ordinary and typical facets of America during the examined era, allowing for a more precise exposition of distinct processes within American society during the mid-20th century, encompassing women's everyday life.

The problem statement and research model constitute merely the initial stage of an extensive scientific undertaking. Presently, the author has amassed over 30 oral memoirs from individuals residing in these cities, scrutinized diverse source types (local periodicals, city maps, brochures about new residences, family photo albums, etc.). Collectively, these resources will constitute the foundation for the subsequent phase of the study, to be documented through new publications within Russian-American scholarly platforms.

References

Anderson 2005 — Anderson D.M. Levittown is Burning! the 1979 Levittown, Pennsylvania, Gas Line Riot and the Decline of the Blue-Collar American Dream // Labor: Studies in Working Class History of the Americas. 2005. Vol. 2 issue 3. P. 47-65.

Baxandall, Ewen 1990 — Baxandall R., Ewen E. Picture Windows: the Changing Role of Women in the Suburbs, 1945-2000 // Long Island Historical Journal. 1990. Vol. 3, no. 1. P. 89-108.

Brown 2015 — Brown K. Plutopia: Nuclear Families, Atomic Cities, and the Great Soviet and American Plutonium Disasters. Oxford University Press, 2015.

Clarke 1994 — Clarke A. "Parties Are the Answer": Gender, Modernity and Material Culture // UCLA Historical Journal. 1994. Vol. 14, P. 155-171.

England 1993 — England K.V.L. Changing Suburbs, Changing Women: Geographic Perspectives on Suburban Women and Suburbanization // Frontiers: a Journal of Women Studies. 1993. Vol. 14, no. 1. P. 24-43.

Fava 1979 — Fava S.F. Changing suburban images: is the bloom off the rose? // New York Affairs. 1979. Vol. 5 issue 4. P. 55-65.

Fava 1985 — Fava S.F. Residential Preferences in the Suburban Era: a New Look? // Sociological Focus. 1985. Vol. 18 (2). P. 109-117.

Giles 2004 — Giles J. Salon and Suburbia: Domestic Identity, Social Strata, Feminism, and Modernity. NY: Berg, 2004.

Hagood 2011 — Hagood C. Rethinking the Nuclear Family: Judith Merril's *Shadow on the Hearth* and Domestic Science Fiction // Women's Studies. 2011.Vol. 40, issue 8. P. 1006-1029.

Hammond 2002 — Hammond Jeffrey Ohio States: a Twentieth-Century Midwestern. Kent, Ohio: Kent State University Press. 2002.

Hartranft 1992 — Hartranft L.B. The Ninth Decade: Six Central Ohio Women. Doctoral dissertation, Ohio State University. 1992.

Hesford 2005 — Hesford V. Patriotic Perversions: Patricia Highsmith's Queer Vision of Cold War America in the Price of Salt, the Blunderer, and Deep Water // Women's Studies Quarterly. 2005. Vol. 33 issue 3/4. P. 215-233.

Hirdman 1991 — Hirdman H. The Gender System // Andreasen T. et al. (eds.). Moving On: New Perspectives on the Women's Movement. Aarhus, 1991. P. 187-207.

Laslett, Brenner 1989 — Laslett B., Brenner J. Gender and Social Reproduction: Historical Perspective // Annual Review of Sociology. 1989. Vol. 15. P. 381-404.

Markusen 1978 – Markusen A.R. Class, Rent and Sectoral Conflict: Uneven Development in Western U.S. Boomtowns // Review of Radical Political Economics. 1978. Vol. 10 issue 3. P. 117-129.

Markusen 1980 — Markusen A.R. How Real-World Work, Advocacy, and Political Economy Strengthen Planning Research and Practice // Journal of Women in Culture & Society. 1980. Vol. 5 issue 3. P. 23-44.

Markusen 1981 — Markusen A.R. City Spatial Structure, Women's Household Work, and National Urban Policy // Simpson C.R. et al. (eds.). Women in the American City. Chicago: University of Chicago Press, 1981.

Markusen 1989 — Markusen A.R. Cold War Economics (cover story) // Bulletin of the Atomic Scientists. 1989. Vol. 45 issue 1. P. 41.

Miller 1981 — Miller Z. Suburb: neighborhood and community in Forest Park, Ohio, 1935-1976. Knoxville: University of Tennessee Press, 1981.

Mitchell 1999 — Mitchell M. When Women Get Together: Black Women, Working Women, and History. // Radical History Review. 1999. Issue 73. P. 172.

Pateman 1998 — Pateman C. The Sexual Contract. Stanford, 1998.

Pushkareva 2019 — Pushkareva N.L. Peculiarities of memory about women's social past and the work of a historian // Bulletin of the Peoples' Friendship University of Russia. Series: Historical Sciences. 2019. Vol. 18. No. 2. P. 206-213.

Rubin 1979 — Rubin M. Debunking the Myth: Working Women in Suburbia // New York Affairs. 1979. Vol. 5 issue 4. P. 78-83.

Saegart 1981 — Saegart S. Suburbs: Polarized Ideas, Contradictory Realities // C.R. Simpson et al. (eds.). Women in the American City. Chicago: University of Chicago. 1981.

Strivers 2000 — Stivers C. Bureau Men, Settlement Women: Constructing Public Administration in the Progressive Era. University Press of Kansas, 2000.

Sturgis 1986 — Sturgis C. How're You Gonna Keep'em Down on the Farm? Rural Women and the Urban model in Utah // Agricultural History. 1986. Vol. 60 issue 2. P. 182-199.

Van Maanen 2011 — Van Maanen J. Tales of the Field on Writing Ethnography. 2nd ed. 2011.

Veremenko, Lyubichanovsky 2019 — Veremenko V.A., Lyubichankovsky S.V. From N.L. Pushkareva to N.L. Pushkareva: modern historiography of the history of women's everyday life in Russia // Bulletin of the Perm University. Series: History. 2019. No. 3(46). P. 85-94.

Walker 1985 — Walker N. Humor and Gender Roles: the Funny Feminism of the Post-World War II Suburbs. // American Quarterly. 1985. Vol. 37 issue 1. P. 98-113.

Warren, Hackney 2000 — Warren C., Hackney J. Gender Issues in Ethnography. 2nd ed. V. 9. 2000.

Wolfinger 2012 — Wolfinger J. The American Dream—For All Americans: Race, Politics, and the Campaign to Desegregate Levittown // Journal of Urban History. 2012. Vol. 38 issue 3. P. 430-451.

Zhidchenko 2016 — Zhidchenko A.V. History of My City: Historical and Cultural Space of New Cities and Urban Areas of Russia in the Middle of the 20th Century. Omsk: Amfora, 2016.

Evolution of Representation of Slavery in the 20th – 21st Centuries American Films: Historical and Cultural Context

Valentina N. Bryndina

This paper focuses on the evolution of slavery representation in 20th – 21st century American films through an analysis of films such as *the Birth of a Nation* (1916 and 2015) and *Roots* (1977 and 2016). This paper investigates how the images of "planter" and "slave" and the relationship between them, changed over time. Comparative analysis of the films made throughout the 20th century and their modern remakes shows how the storyline changed and how these changes were conditioned by the historical and cultural context of the time.

Early 20th century and *the Birth of a Nation*

The Birth of a Nation was directed by David Wark Griffith in 1915 and was not accidentally chosen as the starting point of this paper. Until 1915, there were several common characters of African

Americans in the films. First, there were comic characters who danced, ate watermelons, or bathed black babies (Urwand: 2018). Second, there were characters of "faithful souls" such as Uncle Tom and Mammy. However, in his films, especially *the Birth of a Nation*, Griffith created two totally negative images of African Americans: the tragic mulatto and the brutal black buck. They are no longer funny. in Griffith's films, they became dangerous.

Griffith used three varieties of black. The first were the "faithful souls", a mammy and an uncle Tom, who remain with the Cameron family throughout and staunchly defend them from the rebels. Griffith's second variety was the brutal black buck; this type could likewise be divided into two categories: black brutes and black bucks – black brutes, which commit lawlessness, kill, rape, or rob. These are unnamed characters. Bucks are always big, bad niggers, oversexed and savage, violent, and frenzied as they lust white flesh. Lynch, the mulatto, and Gus, the renegade, fall into this category.

The prewar South is shown idealistically in Griffith's picture. The "correctness" and "naturalness" of the relationship between planters and slaves are emphasized. Civil war and subsequent reconstruction destroyed the world where everything was in its place. Griffith's film was divided into two parts. The watershed is the Civil War, which divided the world into before and after. At the center of the plot are two families: the Stonemans and the Camerons. During the war years, the Stonemans supported the North and the Camerons supported the South. The decline and excess of freed slaves after the Civil War are shown. The creation of the Ku Klux Klan and the unification of the North and South against a common enemy, former slaves, ended lawlessness. The wedding between Stonemans and Camerons symbolizes the union between the North and South and the birth of the nation.

The planters are depicted in the film as noble, honest, and brave. They are gallant with women and are temperate. The film's white heroines are romantic, tender, and defenseless. The relationship with the slaves is shown idealistically. Slaves, on the other hand, walk in the background; they are either plantation workers, servants, or crowds on the street; that is, they are impersonal and have no names. Only servants are shown positively–they symbolize a devoted slave who stays with his master until the very end (Uncle Tom and Mammy). There are also two negative characters on the screen. They are just the new stereotypical heroes Griffith brought to the world of cinema. The first is the tragic mulatto Lynch, who is shown to be crazy. He forces the daughter of the Stonemans, Elsie, to marry him. Another black hero is a black male, Gus, who was a former slave. He is chasing the daughter of the Camerons, Flora, and is thrown off a cliff because she does not want to be defamed. Both characters personify intemperance and excess. Throughout the film, we observe the danger of the "black menace", from which there is only one salvation, the Ku Klux Klan. in other words, slaves are opposed to planters. They are not noble, cowardly or intemperate. Black women are portrayed as unattractive.

This film has raised public awareness. The National Association for the Advancement of Colored People (NAACP) which was created in 1909 advocated film ban or censorship of racial slander which was represented in it (Berry 2009: 14)*. in New York, the film was banned for a while, and it was also refused license for exhibition in Connecticut, Illinois, Kansas, Massachusetts, Minnesota, New Jersey, Wisconsin, Ohio, and many other states (Noble 1970: 39). Nevertheless, despite all the public actions taken against the film, *the Birth of a Nation* was an enormous financial success, establishing D.W. Griffith as the greatest film director of his time and exerting considerable

* See. Cripps Thomas R. The Reaction of the Negro to the Motion Picture Birth of a Nation. *The Historian*. Vol. 25. No. 3. 1963. Pp. 344–362.

influence on millions of people who saw it, and also leading to the rebirth of Ku Klux Klan in 1915*.

The Birth of a Nation was the highest-grossing film of its time, surpassed only by the 1939 release of *Gone with the Wind*. Seeing its success, many Hollywood producers undertook projects with a similar anti-Black theme (Bogle 2001: 17). Interestingly, since Griffith, no director has used such negative images of African Americans. Over time, Black actors started to get comedy roles.

Impact of the Civil Rights Movement

Civil Rights Movement in the 1970s had an impact on films related to the issue of slavery. Although the devoted servants — Uncle Tom and Mammy — remained on the screen, they obtained a different connotation. Their exaggerated devotion was due to the desire to protect their loved ones and not to satisfaction with the system of slavery. Griffith's negative heroes left this stage completely. The unattractiveness of an African American woman was no longer emphasized; on the contrary, the film reflected the problem of white violence against beautiful black slaves. Humility and acceptance of fate were replaced by a desire for freedom and a struggle for one's own identity. White heroes were no longer portrayed as ideals. in the films, the idealized depiction of the South was replaced by depictions of the horrors of slavery. Films of the 1970s were problematic, which we discuss in more detail below. As Donald Bogle, author of *Toms, Coons, Mulattoes, Mammies, and Bucks: An Interpretive History of Blacks in American Films*, notes: "No period in the history of Black cinema has been as energetic and important as the 1970s. More and more Black actors and actresses were acting in films [...] For the first

* See. Simcovitch 1972.

time, in the history of film studios, films aimed at Black audiences began to be created" (Bogle 2001: 232). The 1977 ABC series *Roots* is a prime example of this trend.

Miniseries *Roots* aired on ABC in January 1977. It was based on Alex Haley's 1976 novel *Roots: the Saga of an American Family*. The miniseries is about the fight for freedom and the identity waged by several generations of Kunta Kinte's family. As Jesse Jackson, an African American human rights activist stated: "Haley made a history talk. He lit up the long night of slavery. He gave our grandparents a personhood. He gave roots to the rootless" (Bogle 2001: 50). in the 1970s, both the novel and the film were influenced by the spirit of the Civil Rights Movement. Unlike previous films related to slavery, *Roots* was about African Americans' struggles against slavery and inequality. The film gave African Americans their own hero represented by the main character of Kunta Kinte.

Changes in storyline and their interpretation

1. in the 1977 film, Kunta's birthplace in Africa was shown to be a small village, Juffure, which did not have a long history. The life in Africa has been simplified. The 2016 film began with the following prologues:

> There was once a rich and sophisticated city named Juffure, in the Mandinka kingdom in West Africa. It is located on the banks of Cambibolongo, the great river of Gambia. Like the Greeks, Romans, and Hebrews, Mandinka kept the slaves as servants. Some slaves married these families, whereas others paid ransoms to be free. Subsequently, Europeans arrived on great sailing ships. Some Mandinka were corrupted by European guns and gold, creating a violent market for slaves; however, many Africans who fought European plundering suffered brutal reprisals.

Thus, we see that in 2016 film Juffure, on the contrary, had a long history and was compared with ancient civilizations.

2. in the 1977 film, the clothing of Juffure's inhabitants was simple. in the 2016 film, we can see Arab influence on it. in the remake, however, the connection with Islamic civilization is emphasized through clothes and Kunta's passionate desire to study in Timbuktu.

3. in the 2016 film, we notice that some positive white characters have gone, for example, the Capitan of a slave ship, Mr. Davies, and the white couple who joined Kunta's family in the last episode. in the 1977 film, these characters denote two problems. Capitan Davies discusses the problem of slavery; he is against this cruel system and believes that slavery is abnormal. The white couple, in turn, underlines the possibility of peaceful blacks' and whites' coexistence after the Civil War.

4. Some characters that were neutral in the 1977 film, such as the capitan's mate Mr. Slider, the brother of Kunta's master Dr. John Reynolds and the master of Kunta's grandson, Sam Harvey, acquire some negative characteristics in the 2016 version. Some characters negative in the original film, such as the overseer in Reynold's plantation and the master of Kunta's daughter, Tom Moore (Tome Lea in the remake), are shown to be more violent.

5. There are many murders in *Roots*. Interestingly, some characters who died of natural causes in the original version, such as Fiddler and Noah, in 2016 film were sold by theirs master for their attempt to run away and were killed by the whites.

6. in *Roots* of 2016, we see more dramatic scenes such as whipping, forced family separation, and rapes. Generally, the remake is crueller than the original version.

Thus, we can conclude that in modern remake, some positive white characters were removed, whereas some neutral white characters are attributed with more negative features. They are obsessed with Black women, greedy, cowardly and cruel. There are many murders and violence in the *Roots* remake. in the 2016 film, we notice how the antagonism between the slaves and the planters increased, while issues such as slavery abnormality and the peaceful coexistence of Blacks and whites are replaced by violence.

The Birth of a Nation: new meanings

Finally, let's consider *the Birth of a Nation* (2015) that tells the story of Nat Turner's 1831 rebellion and Nat's life. Although it is not a remake of the 1915 film of the same name, the director and performer of the protagonist role, Nate Parker, noted in an interview with the online media Filmmaker that his film is a response to the 1915 film. He remarked that "Addressing Griffith's Birth of a Nation is one of the many steps necessary in treating this disease. Griffith's film relied heavily on racist propaganda to evoke fear and desperation as a tool to solidify white supremacy as the lifeblood of American sustenance. Not only did this film motivate the massive resurgence of the terror group the Ku Klux Klan and the carnage exacted against people of African descent, it served as the foundation of the film industry we know today" (Rezayazdi 2016). Second, this film puts a new meaning into the *Birth of a Nation* and its example clearly shows how trends have changed over the past century. What has changed?

1. in the foreground, are the slaves.

2. Planters: Minor characters shown as cruel drunkards. The only one is shown to be kind and benevolent, as Nate's master still crosses the line because of his own weakness. in a quest to restore his reputation among wealthy planters, he gives the wife of one of his slaves to a guest.

3. a new meaning for the *Birth of a Nation*. The uprising was a sign of the emergence of self-consciousness and the birth of the African American nation.

4. Emphasis on the experiences and courage of the protagonist, his desire for freedom.

5. The film is violent.

The relationship between "slaves" and "planters" is unequivocally unequal; there is no place for caring and mutual respect
in them.

Conclusion

Thus, we can conclude the following. in the films of the early 20th
century, slavery was portrayed as a "natural" and "correct" system; then, in the 1970s, the horrors of slavery are already depicted. The films of the 2010s, on the other hand, strongly condemn
the slavery system.

The relationship between slaves and planters is becoming
to be portrayed in a more multifaceted way, from an unequivocally idealistic perspective. Films of the 1970s gave examples
of both the cruel treatment of planters with their slaves and
the possibility of planters caring for their slaves and, in general,
peaceful relations with one another. in the films of the 2010s,
the relationship between "slaves" and "planters", with rare ex-
ceptions, is shown negatively, their antagonism intensifies.

We also see a trend towards the emergence of an increasing
number of negative "white" heroes. As seen in the modern remakes of films of the 1970s. Positive white heroes were either
completely removed or their negative sides were emphasized.
African American characters, on the other hand, are acquiring
increasingly positive qualities from the unequivocally negative
images in the films of the early 20th century. They have increasingly been portrayed as heroes and martyrs. a prime example
is the 2015 *the Birth of a Nation.*

Films of the 2010s are cruel, and they have more murders
and torture. Unlike the films of the 1970s, which raised such

issues as the "naturalness" of the slavery system, the possibility of a peaceful existence of planters and former slaves, and the problem of segregation, modern remakes lose this problematic.

References

Berry 2009 — Berry E.F. a Comparative Study of African American Representations in Film from Original to Remake as Influenced by the Civil Rights Movement. University of Maine, 2009.

Bogle 2001 — Bogle D. Toms, Coons, Mulattoes, Mammies, and Bucks: An Interpretive History of Blacks in American Films. Continuum, 2001.

Cripps 1963 — Cripps T.R. The Reaction of the Negro to the Motion Picture *Birth of a Nation* // the Historian. 1963. Vol. 25. no. 3. P. 344–362.

Noble 1970 — Noble P. The Negro in films. Arno Press, 1970.

Rezayazdi 2023 — Rezayazdi S. Five Questions with *The Birth of a Nation* **Director Nate Parker** // Filmmaker. 25.01.2016. URL: https://filmmakermagazine.com/97103-five-questions-with-the-birth-of-a-nation-director-nate-parker/#.YJzzLOomw2y (Date of access: 05.05.2023).

Simcovitch 1972 — Simcovitch M. The Impact of Griffith's *Birth of a Nation* on the Modern Ku Klux Klan // Journal of Popular Film. 1972. Vol. 1 no. 1. P. 45–54.

Urwand 2018 — Urwand B. The Black Image on the White Screen: Representations of African Americans from the Origins of Cinema to *The Birth of a Nation* // Journal of American Studies. 2018. Vol. 52 no. 1. P. 45 – 64.

ANTHROPOLOGY ACROSS BORDERS AND LIMITS: 1ST INDEPENDENT RESEARCH NETWORK SHEETS

(PROCEEDINGS FROM THE 3RD-5TH RUSSIAN-AMERICAN RESEARCH NEXUS FORUMS)

Design by Lizaveta V. Bogdanovskaya